Bryn Mawr Latin Commentaries

Apuleius
Metamorphoses Book III

William Turpin

Thomas Library
Bryn Mawr College
Bryn Mawr, Pennsylvania

The Bryn Mawr Latin Commentaries are supported by a generous grant from the Division of Education Programs of the National Endowment for the Humanities

Copyright ©2002 by **Bryn Mawr Commentaries**

Manufactured in the United States of America
ISBN 0-929524-98-5
Printed and distributed by
Bryn Mawr Commentaries
Thomas Library
Bryn Mawr College
101 North Merion Avenue
Bryn Mawr, PA 19010-2899

Bryn Mawr Latin Commentaries

Editors

Julia Haig Gaisser
Bryn Mawr College

James J. O'Donnell
University of Pennsylvania

The purpose of the Bryn Mawr Latin Commentaries is to make a wide range of classical and post-classical authors accessible to the intermediate student. Each commentary provides the minimum grammatical and lexical information necessary for a first reading of the text.

Preface

This commentary is intended simply to make Book III of the *Metamorphoses* more accessible to new readers. It owes a great deal to the learned commentary of R. T. van der Paardt, and has been much improved by the watchful eye of Julia Gaisser. I am also grateful to an able Swarthmore student, Daniel Koltonski, for his careful proofreading.

Introduction

We do not know Apuleius' full name. He was born about 125 A.D., in the Numidian city of Madaura (modern M'Daourouch, in western Algeria). After a philosophical and rhetorical education in Carthage and Athens, he travelled in the Greek east and to Rome as a professional rhetorician. In 156 (probably), when detained by illness at Oea (modern Tripoli, in Libya), he married a wealthy widow named Pudentilla. The marriage was resented by some of the lady's relatives, who charged Apuleius with winning his bride through magic; Apuleius' successful defense speech, the *Apology*, provides good evidence for his learning and his rhetorical skill. He appears to have lived subsequently in Carthage, where in the 160's he gave rhetorical displays and philosophic lectures; extracts of these speeches are preserved in his *Florida*. Other surviving works include a speech concerning Socrates, the *De deo Socratis*, and perhaps two philosophic treatises, the *De dogmate Platonis* and the Aristotelian *De mundo*, though his authorship of these works is disputed. Lost works include a version of Plato's *Phaedo*, speeches, poems, and treatises on astronomy, music, arithmetic, zoology, agriculture, medicine, politics and history, as well as another novel. We do not know when Apuleius died; nothing is heard of him after 170.

The *Metamorphoses* (also known as *The Golden Ass*) is the only Latin novel to have survived complete. It consists of eleven books, in which the protagonist, Lucius, relates his adventures in the first person. This Lucius, a Greek writing in Latin, is first met on the road to Hypata, in Thessaly, a region famous for witchcraft. In Book I he falls in with some travelers, and because he is fascinated by the occult he persuades one of them to tell a frightening story about witches and their magic. Arriving in Hypata, he finds the house of a man to whom he has an introduction, a notorious miser named Milo. In Book II Lucius runs into a relation of his mother named Byrrhena, who offers him lavish hospitality and warns him that his hostess, Milo's wife Pamphile, is a notorious witch. This merely arouses Lucius' curiosity, so he returns to Milo's house, where he notices the attractions of Milo's slave-girl Fotis, and the two begin a passionate affair. One evening Lucius goes to the house of his relative Byrrhena for an elegant dinner. When the discussion turns to the prevalence of magic in the region, a guest mentions that someone had recently had his face horribly mutilated as result of an encounter with witches. The guests all laugh uproariously at this, and Byrrhena prevails upon the speaker, Thelyphron, to tell his story; Thelyphron does so, and it turns out that he is in fact the person with a mutilated face, concealed now by long hair and a bandaged nose. At the end of the story the guests all laugh once again, and offer a toast to the god Risus (Laughter). Byrrhena explains that on the next day the town of Hypata will celebrate a festival dedicated to Risus, and she invites Lucius to return for another dinner the next evening. She asks him to think of some clever way of honoring Risus, and Lucius promises to try. Returning to Milo's house Lucius encounters what he takes to be a gang of three robbers laying siege to the door, and he kills them.

Lucius' adventures in Book III are odder still. It is not giving away too much to say that Lucius' curiosity about magic results in his astonishing transformation (metamorphosis) into an jackass. The rest of the novel consists largely of Lucius' experiences in this unfortunate state; his adventures are often sexual, and it is important to remember that for the Romans the jackass was notorious not just for stupidity but also for sexual excess. The story of Lucius is interspersed with digressions, of which the most famous is the tale of Cupid and Psyche (*Met.* IV.28-VI.24). After many tribulations and dangers, Lucius is eventually saved by the goddess Isis, and the last book, book XI, is devoted to his religious conversion and salvation.

Lucius' adventures reveal a side of life in the Roman empire that normally gets little attention from ancient authors: he meets brigands, soldiers, itinerant priests, a gardener, a baker, and the baker's wife, who may also be a Christian. The novel is not, of course, intended as an authentic report, but it does offer something of a sense of what life in the Roman empire was actually like, much as *Don Quixote* and *Tristram Shandy* give us at least the illusion that we have experienced the worlds of Cervantes and Sterne.

The central questions raised by the *Metamorphoses* are those of its message and its coherence, and these are in a sense two sides of the same question. Apuleius' novel was preceded by a version of the Lucius story in Greek, by one Lucius of Patrae; this work is lost, but a version attributed to the Greek writer Lucian (born c. 120 A.D.) survives. Lucian's version tells of Lucius' adventures without the digressions (especially the Cupid and Psyche story) and without the intervention of Isis at the end. The question is, then, how much significance to attach to Apuleius' additions. Scholars used to argue that the addition of Book XI, with the Isis ceremony of redemption, was simply a sort of appendix, added to make the bawdiness of Books I-X more acceptable. Most scholars nowadays see the novel as a more carefully constructed whole, but there is much debate about its point. One scholar (Merkelbach) has argued that the book is focussed on the redemption by Isis, and that Books I-X, apparently so antithetical to a religious message of this kind, are in fact an extended allegory about Isis.

Others have argued that even the intervention of Isis is allegorical. One key text for this argument is Plutarch's *De Iside et Osiride*, which explains the Isis cult in Platonic terms. Even more telling is the story of Cupid and Psyche, placed firmly at the center of the book; no one familiar with Plato's *Symposium* will have much difficulty seeing the Platonic aspects of a story about someone named "Soul" and her marriage to, and loss of, "Eros." Equally important, perhaps, is the tradition of allegorizing Plato's own dialogues (including the *Symposium*) in the writings of Middle Platonism, with which Apuleius was contemporary, and the mystical approach to basic concepts such as Eros found in Neoplatonic writers such as Plotinus (A.D. 205-269/70). Extending the allegory to the main story of Lucius' adventures is not as easy, but there are hints that some aspects of the story, which seem at first to be purely part of the entertainment, in fact have more significance than at first appears: magic, curiosity, and even sexuality turn out to be wrong turnings in philosophy as well as mistakes in Lucius' own life. Whether one can apply this allegorical reading to a detailed reading of the entire novel is less clear, but Book III provides an interesting test case; it is worth considering whether an allegorical reading might not make better sense of the Risus festival, the sex, and the magic.

Apuleius' Latin will seem odd, and in some ways difficult, to students accustomed to the prose of Cicero and Caesar, or even that of Tacitus and Petronius. This is not usually a matter of syntax; although Apuleius' syntax has a number of unclassical features, they usually have some parallels in texts of the classical period, and they in any case rarely cause difficulties. The problems stem, rather, from Apuleius' deliberate creation of a Latin that keeps the reader constantly on edge. In the first place, Apuleius uses an extraordinarily rich vocabulary; he invents new words, gives new meanings to familiar words, and uses words in their original or out-of-date meanings. Even more important, however, is his tendency to load sentences with phrase after phrase, often describing events in what seems to us excessive detail. But unlike writers who are wordy from sheer laziness, Apuleius adds language out of a kind of exuberant creativity. As an African, Apuleius may well have had as his first language Punic, and it has been suggested that his pushing of the traditional limits of Latin prose has something in common with the verbal creativity of Joseph Conrad or Vladimir Nabokov, for whom

English was a second or third language. However that may be, Conrad at least seems a helpful parallel, since the key for both Apuleius and Conrad is (in my view) to be patient about making progress with the story, and to enjoy the language for its own sake.

It is probably impossible to appreciate Apuleius in Latin without reading him aloud. The importance of the oral dimension to Apuleius is confirmed by his extensive use of standard metrical cadences (*clausulae*) to bring his sentences to an end. The Romans did not usually make use of punctuation, in part no doubt because literature was normally read aloud rather than silently. The use of *clausulae* allowed audiences to recognize the end of a sentence, or at least an end that really mattered, since the metrical forms were familiar and emphatic (for more on *clausulae* see the *Oxford Classical Dictionary*, 3rd edition, under "prose-rhythm, Latin"). It has been calculated that Apuleius used *clausulae* to end 92.5% of all his sentences, which is a degree of consistency almost without parallel in Latin prose. His favorite *clausulae* are:

$$- \cup - - \cup \text{ X}$$
$$- \cup - - \text{ X}$$
$$- \cup - \text{ X}$$

In all these cases long syllables can be resolved into two shorts.

The Latin text printed here is based primarily on those of van der Paardt and Hanson; the numbering of sections (usually sentences) within each chapter is that of Robertson. My text makes no claims for innovation, except that I have provided more punctuation than is common in the standard texts. Apuleius' basic style is paratactic: his more elaborate sentences tend to pile phrase upon phrase. It is often not easy for the English reader to see where one phrase ends and another begins, and I have added a number of commas, and occasionally parentheses and dashes, simply to help in translation.

A Short Bibliography for Apuleius, Metamorphoses III

1. Texts.
   J. Arthur Hanson, *Apuleius, Metamorphoses* (two volumes). Cambridge, 1989 (Loeb Classical Library) [with English translation].
   D. S. Robertson, *Apulée, Les Métamorphoses, Tome I (Livres I-III)*. Paris, 1965. [with French translation].
   R. T. van der Paardt, L. *Apuleius Madaurensis, The Metamorphoses: A commentary on Book III with text and introduction*. Amsterdam, 1971. [a very thorough and detailed commentary].

2. Translations of the *Metamorphoses*.
   E. J. Kenney, Apuleius, *The Golden Ass, or Metamorphoses*. Penguin, 1999.
   Robert Graves, *The Golden Ass*. New York, 1951. [very readable, but unreliable, and lacks book and chapter numbers].
   Jack Lindsay, *The Golden Ass*. Bloomington, 1960.
   P. G. Walsh, *Apuleius, Golden Ass*. Oxford, 1994.
   See also the Loeb edition by J. Arthur Hanson.

3. Introductions to the *Metamorphoses*.
   E. L. Bowie and S. J. Harrison, "The Romance of the Novel," *Journal of Roman Studies* 83 (1993), 159-178 [bibliographic survey of work on the Greek and Latin novel].
   E. J. Kenney, *Apuleius, Cupid and Psyche*. Cambridge, 1990. [an excellent introduction, esp. for Apuleius' Latin].
   P. G. Walsh, "Apuleius," in E. J. Kenney, ed., *The Cambridge History of Classical Literature, II: Latin Literature*. Cambridge, 1982, pp. 774-786.
   There are also excellent introductions by Walsh and Kenney in their translations.

4. Studies of the *Metamorphoses* in general.
   Ellen D. Finkelpearl, *Metamorphosis of Language in Apuleius: A Study of Allusion in the Novel*. Ann Arbor, 1998.
   B. L. Hijmans and R. T. van der Paardt, eds., *Aspects of Apuleius' Golden Ass*, Groningen, 1978.
   R. Merkelbach, *Roman und Mysterium in der Antike*. Munich, 1962.
   Fergus Millar, "The World of the Golden Ass," *Journal of Roman Studies* 71 (1981), 63-75, rpt. in S. J. Harrison, ed., *Oxford Readings in the Roman Novel*. Oxford, 1999. pp. 247-268 [on Apuleius as a source for Roman social history]
   Carl C. Schlam, *The Metamorphoses of Apuleius: On Making an Ass of Oneself*. Chapel Hill, 1992.
   Nancy Shumate, *Crisis and Conversion in Apuleius' Metamorphoses*. Ann Arbor, 1996.

James Tatum, *Apuleius and The Golden Ass*. Ithaca, 1979.
P. G. Walsh, *The Roman Novel: the 'Satyricon' of Petronius and the Metamorphoses of Apuleius*. Cambridge, 1970.
John J. Winkler, *Auctor & Actor: A Narratological Reading of Apuleius's Golden Ass*. Berkeley, 1985.
Antonie Wlossok, "On the Unity of Apuleius' Metamorphoses," in S. J. Harrison, ed., *Oxford Readings in the Roman Novel*. Oxford, 1999. pp. 142-156.

5. Related ancient texts.
Lucian, "Lucius, or The Ass," translated by M. D. Macleod, *Lucian*, vol. VIII (Loeb Classical Library).
Plutarch, *De Iside et Osiride*, translated by Frank Cole Babbitt, *Plutarch's Moralia*, vol. V (1962) (Loeb Classical Library).

6. Specific Topics relating to Book III.
Joseph G. DeFilippo, "Curiositas and the Platonism of Apuleius' Golden Ass," *American Journal of Philology* 111 (1990), 471-492, rpt. in S. J. Harrison, ed., *Oxford Readings in the Roman Novel*. Oxford, 1999. pp. 269-289.
R. de Smet, "The Erotic Adventures of Lucius and Photis in Apuleius' *Metamorphoses*," *Latomus* 46 (1987), 613-623.
J. Englert and T. Long, "Functions of Hair in Apuleius' *Metamorphoses*," *Classical Journal* 68 (1972/73), 236-239.
J. L. Penwill, "Slavish Pleasures and Profitless Curiosity," *Ramus* 4 (1975), 49-82.
G. Sandy, "Knowledge and Curiosity in Apuleius' Metamorphoses," *Latomus* 31 (1972), 179-183.

7. The Language of Apuleius (and vulgar Latin in general)
L. Callebat, *Sermo cotidianus dans les Métamorphoses d'Apulée*. Caen, 1968.
Mario Pei, *The Story of Latin and the Romance Languages*. New York, 1976.

Abbreviations

AG   Allen and Greenough, New Latin Grammar, rpt. New Rochelle, 1983.
OLD Oxford Latin Dictionary, ed. P. G. W. Glare, Oxford 1982.
sc. scilicet (literally "no doubt"), i.e. "understand."
< > in the Latin text encloses words that are not in the ancient manuscripts but have been supplied by modern editors.

Metamorphoses III

1. (1) Commodum punicantibus phaleris Aurora roseum quatiens lacertum caelum inequitabat, et me securae quieti revulsum nox diei reddidit. (2) aestus invadit animum vesperni recordatione facinoris. complicitis denique pedibus, ac palmulis in alternas digitorum vicissitudines super genua conexis, sic grabatum cossim insidens ubertim flebam, iam forum ac iudicia, iam sententiam, ipsum denique carnificem imaginabundus. (3) "An mihi quisquam tam mitis tamque benivolus iudex obtinget, qui me trinae caedis cruore perlitum et tot civium sanguine delibutum innocentem pronuntiare poterit? (4) hanc illam mihi gloriosam peregrinationem fore Chaldaeus Diophanes obstinate praedicabat." (5) haec identidem mecum replicans, fortunas meas heiulabam. quati fores interdum et frequenti clamore ianuae nostrae perstrepi.

2. (1) Nec mora, cum—magna inruptione patefactis aedibus—magistratibus eorumque ministris et turbae miscellaneae cuncta completa, statimque lictores duo de iussu magistratuum immissa manu trahere me sane non renitentem occipiunt. (2) ac dum primum angiportum insistimus, statim civitas omnis in populum effusa mira densitate nos insequitur. (3) et quamquam, capite in terram—immo ad ipsos inferos—iam deiecto, maestus incederem, obliquato tamen aspectu rem admirationis maximae conspicio: (4) nam inter tot milia populi circumsedentis nemo prorsum, qui non risu dirumperetur, aderat. (5) tandem—pererratis plateis omnibus, et in modum eorum, qui lustralibus piamentis minas portentorum hostiis circumforaneis expiant, circumductus angulatim—forum eiusque tribunal adstituor. (6) iamque sublimo suggestu magistratibus residentibus, iam praecone publico silentium clamante, repente cuncti consona voce flagitant, propter coetus multitudinem, quae pressurae nimia densitate periclitaretur, iudicium tantum theatro redderetur. (7) nec mora, cum passim populus procurrens caveae conseptum mira celeritate conplevit; (8) aditus etiam et tectum omne fartim stipaverant, plerique columnis implexi, alii statuis dependuli, nonnulli per fenestras et lacunaria semiconspicui, miro tamen omnes studio visendi pericula salutis neclegebant. (9) tunc me per proscaenium medium velut quandam victimam publica ministeria producunt et orchestrae mediae sistunt.

3. (1) Sic rursum praeconis amplo boatu citatus, accusator quidam senior exsurgit et—ad dicendi spatium vasculo quodam in vicem coli graciliter fistulato ac per hoc guttatim defluo infusa aqua—populum sic adorat:

(2) "Neque parva res ac praecipue pacem civitatis cunctae respiciens et exemplo serio profutura tractatur, Quirites sanctissimi. (3) quare magis congruit sedulo singulos atque universos vos pro dignitate publica providere, ne nefarius homicida tot caedium lanienam, quam cruenter exercuit, inpune commisserit. (4) nec me putetis privatis simultatibus instinctum odio proprio saevire. sum namque nocturnae custodiae praefectus, nec in hodiernum credo quemquam pervigilem diligentiam meam culpare posse.

(5) "Rem denique ipsam, et quae nocte gesta sunt, cum fide perferam. nam cum fere iam tertia vigilia scrupulosa diligentia cunctae civitatis ostiatim singula considerans circumirem, (6) conspicio istum crudelissimum iuvenem mucrone destricto passim caedibus operantem, iamque tris numero saevitia eius interemptos ante pedes ipsius spirantes adhuc, corporibus in multo sanguine palpitantes. (7) et ipse quidem, conscientia tanti facinoris merito permotus, statim profugit et, in domum quandam praesidio tenebrarum elapsus, perpetem noctem delituit. (8) sed providentia deum, quae nihil impunitum nocentibus permittit, priusquam iste clandestinis itineribus elaberetur, mane praestolatus ad gravissimum iudicii vestri sacramentum eum curavi perducere. (9) habetis itaque reum tot caedibus impiatum, reum coram deprensum, reum peregrinum. constanter itaque in hominem alienum ferte sententias de eo crimine, quod etiam in vestrum civem severiter vindicaretis."

4. (1) Sic profatus accusator acerrimus immanem vocem repressit. ac me statim praeco, si quid ad ea respondere vellem, iubebat incipere. (2) at ego nihil tunc temporis amplius quam flere poteram, non tam hercules truculentam accusationem intuens quam meam miseram conscientiam. sed tamen oborta divinitus audacia sic ad illa:

(3) "Nec ipse ignoro, quam sit arduum—trinis civium corporibus expositis—eum qui caedis arguatur, quamvis vera dicat et de facto confiteatur ultro, (4) tamen tantae multitudini, quod sit innocens, persuadere. set si paulisper audientiam publica mihi tribuerit humanitas, facile vos edocebo me discrimen capitis non meo merito, sed rationabilis indignationis eventu fortuito tantam criminis invidiam frustra sustinere.

5. (1) "Nam cum a cena me serius aliquanto reciperem, potulentus alioquin—quod plane verum crimen meum non diffitebor—ante ipsas fores hospitii (ad bonum autem Milonem civem vestrum devorto) (2) video quosdam saevissimos latrones aditum temptantes et domus ianuas cardinibus obtortis evellere gestientes, claustrisque omnibus (quae accuratissime adfixa fuerant) violenter evulsis, secum iam de inhabitantium exitio deliberantes. (3) unus denique et manu promptior et corpore vastior his adfatibus et ceteros incitabat: (4) 'heus pueri, quam maribus animis et viribus alacribus dormientes adgrediamur. omnis cunctatio, ignavia omnis facessat e pectore: stricto mucrone per totam domum caedes ambulet. (5) qui sopitus iacebit, trucidetur; qui repugnare temptaverit, feriatur. sic salvi recedemus, si salvum in domo neminem reliquerimus.' (6) fateor, Quirites, extremos latrones—boni civis officium arbitratus, simul et eximie metuens et hospitibus meis et mihi— (7) gladiolo, qui me propter huiusmodi pericula comitabatur, armatus fugare atque proterrere eos adgressus sum. (8) at illi barbari prorsus et immanes homines neque fugam capessunt et, cum me viderent in ferro, tamen audaciter resistunt.

6. (1) "Dirigitur proeliaris acies. ipse denique dux et signifer ceterorum, validis me viribus adgressus, ilico manibus ambabus capillo adreptum ac retro reflexum effligere lapide gestit. (2) quem dum sibi porrigi flagitat, certa manu percussum feliciter prosterno. ac mox alium pedibus meis mordicus inhaerentem per scapulas ictu temperato tertiumque improvide occurrentem pectore offenso peremo. (3) sic pace vindicata, domoque hospitum ac salute communi protecta, non tam impunem me, verum etiam laudabilem publice credebam fore, qui ne tantillo quidem umquam crimine postulatus, sed probe spectatus apud meos semper innocentiam commodis cunctis antetuleram. (4) nec possum repperire, cur iustae ultionis, qua contra latrones deterrimos commotus sum, nunc istum reatum sustineam, (5) cum nemo possit monstrare vel proprias inter nos inimicitias praecessisse, ac ne omnino mihi notos illos latrones usquam fuisse. vel certe ulla praeda monstretur, cuius cupidine tantum flagitium creditur admissum."

7. (1) Haec profatus, rursum lacrimis obortis porrectisque in preces manibus, per publicam misericordiam, per pignorum caritatem, maestus tunc hos, tunc illos deprecabar. (2) cumque iam humanitate commotos, misericordia fletuum adfectos omnis satis crederem, Solis et Iustitiae testatus oculos, casumque praesentem meum commendans deum providentiae, (3) paulo altius aspectu relato, conspicio prorsus totum populum—risu cachinnabili diffluebant—nec secus illum bonum hospitem parentemque meum Milonem risu maximo

dissolutum. (4) at tunc sic tacitus mecum: "En fides," inquam, "en conscientia; ego quidem pro hospitis salute et homicida sum et reus capitis inducor, at ille non contentus, quod mihi nec adsistendi solacium perhibuit, insuper exitium meum cachinnat."

8. (1) Inter haec, quaedam mulier per medium theatrum lacrimosa et flebilis atra veste contecta, parvulum quendam sinu tolerans, decurrit, ac pone eam anus alia, pannis horridis obsita paribusque maesta fletibus, ramos oleagineos utraeque quatientes, (2) quae circumfusae lectulum, quo peremptorum cadavera contecta fuerant, plangore sublato se lugubriter eiulantes: (3) "Per publicam misericordiam, per commune ius humanitatis," aiunt, "miseremini indigne caesorum iuvenum, nostraeque viduitati ac solitudini de vindicta solacium date. (4) certe parvuli huius in primis annis destituti fortunis succurrite, et de latronis huius sanguine legibus vestris et disciplinae publicae litate."

(5) Post haec magistratus, qui natu maior, adsurgit et ad populum talia: "De scelere quidem, quod serio vindicandum est, nec ipse, qui commisit, potest diffiteri; sed una tantum subsiciva sollicitudo nobis relicta est, ut ceteros socios tanti facinoris requiramus. (6) nec enim veri simile est hominem solitarium tres tam validos evitasse iuvenes. prohinc tormentis veritas eruenda. (7) nam et qui comitabatur eum puer clanculo profugit, et res ad hoc deducta est, ut per quaestionem sceleris sui participes indicet, ut tam dirae factionis funditus formido perematur."

9. (1) Nec mora, cum ritu Graeciensi ignis et rota, cum omne flagrorum genus inferuntur. (2) augetur oppido, immo duplicatur mihi maestitia, quod integro saltim mori non licuerit. (3) sed anus illa, quae fletibus cuncta turbaverat: "Prius," inquit, "optimi cives, quam latronem istum miserorum pignorum meorum peremptorem cruci adfigatis, permittite corpora necatorum revelari, (4) ut, et formae simul et aetatis contemplatione magis magisque ad iustam indignationem arrecti, pro modo facinoris saeviatis."

(5) His dictis adplauditur, et ilico me magistratus ipsum iubet corpora, quae lectulo fuerant posita, mea manu detegere. (6) luctantem me ac diu rennuentem praecedens facinus instaurare nova ostensione, lictores iussu magistratuum quam instantissime compellunt, manum denique ipsam e regione lateris tundentes, in exitium suum super ipsa cadavera porrigunt. (7) evictus tandem necessitate, succumbo et—ingratis licet—abrepto pallio retexi corpora. dii boni, quae facies rei? quod monstrum? quae fortunarum mearum repentina mutatio? (8) quamquam enim iam in peculio Proserpinae et Orci familia numeratus, subito in contrariam faciem obstupefactus

Metamorphoses III

haesi. nec possum novae illius imaginis rationem idoneis verbis expedire. (9) nam cadavera illa iugulatorum hominum erant tres utres inflati variisque secti foraminibus et, ut vespertinum proelium meum recordabar, his locis hiantes, quibus latrones illos vulneraveram.

10. (1) Tunc ille quorundam astu paulisper cohibitus risus libere iam exarsit in plebem. hi gaudii nimietate gratulari, illi dolorem ventris manuum compressione sedare. et certe laetitia delibuti meque respectantes cuncti theatro facessunt. (2) at ego ut primum illam laciniam prenderam, fixus in lapidem, steti gelidus, nihil secus quam una de ceteris theatri statuis vel columnis. (3) nec prius ab inferis emersi, quam Milon hospes accessit, et—iniecta manu—me renitentem, lacrimisque rursum promicantibus crebra singultientem, clementi violentia secum adtraxit, (4) et observatis viae solitudinibus per quosdam amfractus domum suam perduxit, maestumque me atque etiam tunc trepidum variis solatur affatibus. (5) nec tamen indignationem iniuriae, quae inhaeserat altius meo pectori, ullo modo permulcere quivit.

11. (1) Ecce ilico etiam ipsi magistratus cum suis insignibus domum nostram ingressi, talibus me monitis delenire gestiunt: "Neque tuae dignitatis vel etiam prosapiae tuorum ignari sumus, Luci domine; nam et provinciam totam inclitae vestrae familiae nobilitas conplectitur. (2) ac ne istud, quod vehementer ingemescis, contumeliae causa perpessus es. omnem itaque de tuo pectore praesentem tristitudinem mitte et angorem animi depelle. (3) nam lusus iste, quem publice gratissimo deo Risui per annua reverticula sollemniter celebramus, semper commenti novitate florescit. (4) iste deus auctorem et actorem suum propitius ubique comitabitur amanter, nec umquam patietur, ut ex animo doleas, sed frontem tuam serena venustate laetabit adsidue. (5) at tibi civitas omnis pro ista gratia honores egregios obtulit; nam et patronum scribsit et ut in aere stet imago tua decrevit."

(6) Ad haec dicta, sermonis vicem refero: "Tibi quidem," inquam, "splendidissima et unica Thessaliae civitas, honorum talium parem gratiam memini, verum statuas et imagines dignioribus meique maioribus reservare suadeo."

12. (1) Sic pudenter allocutus et paulisper hilaro vultu renidens, quantumque poteram laetiorem me refingens comiter abeuntes magistratus appello. (2) et ecce quidam intro currens famulus: "Rogat te," ait, "tua parens Byrrhena, et convivii cui te sero desponderas iam adpropinquantis admonet." (3) ad haec ego formidans et procul perhorrescens etiam ipsam domum eius, "Quam vellem," inquam, "parens, iussis tuis obsequium commodare, si per fidem liceret id

facere. (4) hospes enim meus Milon, per hodierni diei praesentissimum numen adiurans, effecit, ut eius hodiernae cenae pignerarer, nec ipse discedit nec me digredi patitur. prohinc epulare vadimonium differamus."

(5) Haec adhuc me loquente, manu firmiter iniecta, Milon—iussis balnearibus adsequi—producit ad lavacrum proximum. at ego vitans oculos omnium et, quem ipse fabricaveram, risum obviorum declinans, lateri eius adambulabam obtectus. (6) nec qui laverim, qui terserim, qui domum rursum reverterim, prae rubore memini; sic omnium oculis, nutibus, ac denique manibus denotatus, inpos animi stupebam.

13. (1) Raptim denique paupertina Milonis cenula perfunctus, causatusque capitis acrem dolorem, quem mihi lacrimarum adsiduitas incusserat, concedo—venia facile tributa—cubitum, et abiectus in lectulo meo, quae gesta fuerant, singula maestus recordabar, (2) quoad tandem Fotis mea—dominae suae cubitu procurato—sui longe dissimilis advenit; non enim laeta facie nec sermone dicaculo, sed—vultuosam frontem rugis insurgentibus—adseverabat. (3) cunctanter ac timide denique sermone prolato, "Ego," inquit, "ipsa, confiteor ultro, ego <origo> tibi huius molestiae fui," (4) et, cum dicto, lorum quempiam sinu suo depromit mihique porrigens, "Cape," inquit, "oro te, et de perfida muliere vindictam—immo vero licet maius quodvis supplicium—sume. (5) nec tamen me putes, oro, sponte angorem istum tibi concinnasse. dii mihi melius, quam ut mei causa vel tantillum scrupulum patiare. (6) ac si quid adversi tuum caput respicit, id omne protinus meo luatur sanguine. sed quod alterius rei causa facere iussa sum, mala quadam mea sorte in tuam reccidit iniuriam."

14. (1) Tunc ego familiaris curiositatis admonitus, factique causam delitiscentem nudari gestiens, suscipio: (2) "Omnium quidem nequissimus audacissimusque lorus iste, quem tibi verberandae destinasti, prius a me concisus atque laceratus interibit ipse, quam tuam plumeam lacteamque contingat cutem. (3) sed mihi cum fide memora: quod tuum factum scaevitas consecuta in meum convertit exitium? adiuro enim tuum mihi carissimum caput: nulli me prorsus ac ne tibi quidem ipsi adseveranti posse credere, quod tu quicquam in meam cogitaveris perniciem. (4) porro meditatus innoxios casus incertus vel etiam adversus culpae non potest addicere."

(5) Cum isto fine sermonis oculos Fotidis meae udos ac tremulos et prona libidine marcidos iamiamque semiadopertulos adnixis et sorbillantibus saviis sitienter hauriebam.

15. (1) Sic illa, laetitia recreata, "Patere," inquit, "oro, prius fores cubiculi diligenter obcludam, ne, sermonis elapsi profana petulantia committam grande flagitium." (2) et cum dicto pessulis iniectis, et uncino firmiter immisso, sic ad me reversa colloque meo manibus ambabus inplexa, voce tenui et admodum minuta, (3) "Paveo," inquit, "et formido solide domus huius operta detegere et arcana dominae meae revelare secreta. (4) sed melius de te doctrinaque tua praesumo, qui praeter generosam natalium dignitatem, praeter sublime ingenium, sacris pluribus initiatus profecto nosti sanctam silentii fidem. (5) quaecumque itaque commisero huius religiosi pectoris tui penetralibus, semper haec intra conseptum clausa custodias, oro, et simplicitatem relationis meae tenacitate taciturnitatis tuae remunerare. (6) nam me, quae sola mortalium novi, amor is, quo tibi teneor, indicare compellit. (7) iam scies omnem domus nostrae statum, iam scies erae meae miranda secreta, quibus obaudiunt manes, turbantur sidera, coguntur numina, serviunt elementa. (8) nec umquam magis artis huius violentia nititur, quam cum scitulae formulae iuvenem quempiam libenter aspexit, quod quidem ei solet crebriter evenire.

16. (1) "Nunc etiam adulescentem quendam Boeotium summe decorum efflictim deperit, totasque artis manus, machinas omnes ardenter exercet. (2) audivi vesperi—meis his, inquam, auribus audivi—quod non celerius sol caelo ruisset noctique ad exercendas inlecebras magiae maturius cessisset, ipsi Soli nubilam caliginem et perpetuas tenebras comminantem. (3) hunc iuvenem, cum e balneis rediret ipsa, tonstrinae residentem hesterna die forte conspexit, ac me capillos eius, qui iam caede cultrorum desecti humi diiacebant, clanculo praecipitavit ferre. (4) quos me sedulo furtimque colligentem tonsor invenit, et quod alioquin publicitus maleficae disciplinae perinfames sumus, adreptam inclementer increpat: (5) 'Tune, ultima, non cessas subinde lectorum iuvenum capillamenta surripere? quod scelus nisi tandem desines, magistratibus te constanter obiciam.' (6) et verbum facto secutus, immissa manu scrutatus, e mediis papillis meis iam capillos absconditos iratus abripit. (7) quo gesto graviter adfecta, mecumque reputans dominae meae mores—quod huiusmodi repulsa satis acriter commoveri meque verberare saevissime consuevit—iam de fuga consilium tenebam, sed istud quidem tui contemplatione abieci statim.

17. (1) "Verum cum tristis inde discederem, ne prorsus vacuis manibus redirem, conspicor quendam forficulis adtondentem caprinos utres; (2) quos cum probe constrictos inflatosque et iam pendentis cernerem, capillos eorum humi iacentes flavos ac per hoc illi Boeotio iuveni consimiles plusculos aufero, eosque dominae meae dissimulata veritate trado. (3) sic noctis initio, priusquam cena te reciperes, Pamphile mea iam vecors animi tectum scandulare conscendit, quod altrinsecus aedium patore perflabili nudatum, ad omnes—orientales ceterosque—aspectus pervium, maxime his artibus suis commodatum, secreto colit. (4) priusque apparatu solito instruit feralem officinam: omne genus aromatis, et ignorabiliter lamminis litteratis, et infelicium navium durantibus damnis, (5) defletorum—sepultorum etiam—cadaverum expositis multis admodum membris; hic nares et digiti, illic carnosi clavi pendentium, alibi trucidatorum servatus cruor et extorta dentibus ferarum trunca calvaria.

18. (1) "Tunc decantatis spirantibus fibris, litat vario latice—nunc rore fontano, nunc lacte vaccino, nunc melle montano—libat et mulsa. (2) sic illos capillos in mutuos nexus obditos atque nodatos cum multis odoribus dat vivis carbonibus adolendos. (3) tunc protinus inexpugnabili magicae disciplinae potestate et caeca numinum coactorum violentia, illa corpora, quorum fumabant stridentes capilli, spiritum mutuantur humanum (4) et sentiunt et audiunt et ambulant et, qua nidor suarum ducebat exuviarum, veniunt, et pro illo iuvene Boeotio, aditum gestientes, fores insiliunt: (5) cum ecce crapula madens et improvidae noctis deceptus caligine, audacter mucrone destricto in insani modum Aiacis armatus, (6) non ut ille vivis pecoribus infestus tota laniavit armenta, sed longe fortius, qui tres inflatos caprinos utres exanimasti, (7) ut ego te—prostratis hostibus sine macula sanguinis—non homicidam nunc, sed utricidam amplecterer."

19. (1) Risi lepido sermone Fotidis et in vicem cavillatus, "Ergo igitur iam et ipse possum," inquam, "mihi primam istam virtutis adoriam ad exemplum duodeni laboris Herculei numerare, (2) vel trigemino corpori Geryonis vel triplici formae Cerberi totidem peremptos utres coaequando. (3) sed ut ex animo tibi volens omne delictum, quo me tantis angoribus inplicasti, remittam, praesta quod summis votis expostulo, (4) et dominam tuam, cum aliquid huius divinae disciplinae molitur, ostende: cum deos invocat, certe cum reformatur, videam. sum namque coram magiae noscendae ardentissimus cupitor, (5) quamquam mihi nec ipsa tu videare rerum rudis vel expers. scio istud et plane sentio, cum semper alioquin spretorem matronalium amplexuum sic tuis istis micantibus oculis et rubentibus bucculis et renidentibus crinibus et hiantibus osculis et fraglantibus papillis in servilem modum addictum atque mancipatum teneas volentem. (6) iam denique nec larem requiro nec domuitionem paro et nocte ista nihil antepono."

Metamorphoses III

20. (1) "Quam vellem," inquit illa, "praestare tibi, Luci, quod cupis; sed praeter invidos mores, in solitudinem semper abstrusa et omnium praesentia viduata solet huiusmodi secreta perficere. (2) sed tuum postulatum praeponam periculo meo, idque observatis opportunis temporibus sedulo perficiam, modo, ut initio praefata sum, rei tantae fidem silentiumque tribue."

(3) Sic nobis garrientibus libido mutua et animos simul et membra suscitat. (4) omnibus abiectis amiculis hactenus, denique intecti atque nudati bacchamur in Venerem, cum quidem mihi iam fatigato, de propria liberalitate, Fotis puerile obtulit corollarium; iamque luminibus nostris vigilia marcidis infusus sopor etiam in altum diem nos attinuit.

21. (1) Ad hunc modum transactis voluptarie paucis noctibus, quadam die percita Fotis ac satis trepida me accurrit, indicatque dominam suam, quod nihil etiam tunc in suos amores ceteris artibus promoveret, nocte proxima in avem sese plumaturam, atque ad suum cupitum sic devolaturam; (2) proin memet ad rei tantae speculam caute praepararem. (3) iamque circa primam noctis vigiliam ad illud superius cubiculum suspenso et insono vestigio me perducit ipsa, perque rimam ostiorum quampiam iubet arbitrari, quae sic gesta sunt. (4) iam primum omnibus laciniis se devestit Pamphile, et—arcula quadam reclusa—pyxides plusculas inde depromit, de quis unius operculo remoto atque indidem egesta unguedine diuque palmulis suis adfricta, ab imis unguibus sese totam adusque summos capillos perlinit, multumque cum lucerna secreto conlocuta, membra tremulo succussu quatit. (5) quis leniter fluctuantibus, promicant molles plumulae, crescunt et fortes pinnulae, duratur nasus incurvus, coguntur ungues adunci. (6) fit bubo Pamphile. sic edito stridore querulo, iam sui periclitabunda, paulatim terra resultat; mox in altum sublimata forinsecus totis alis evolat.

22. (1) Et illa quidem magicis suis artibus volens reformatur, at ego nullo decantatus carmine, praesentis tantum facti stupore defixus, quidvis aliud magis videbar esse quam Lucius: (2) sic exterminatus animi, attonitus in amentiam vigilans somniabar; defrictis adeo diu pupulis, an vigilarem, scire quaerebam. (3) tandem denique reversus ad sensum praesentium, adrepta manu Fotidis et admota meis luminibus, (4) "Patere, oro te," inquam, "dum dictat occasio, magno et singulari me adfectionis tuae fructu perfrui, (5) et impertire nobis unctulum indidem—per istas tuas papillas, mea mellitula—tuumque mancipium inremunerabili beneficio sic tibi perpetuo pignera, ac iam perfice, ut meae Veneri Cupido pinnatus adsistam tibi."

(6) "Ain," inquit, "vulpinaris, amasio, meque sponte asceam cruribus meis inlidere compellis? sic inermem vix a lupulis conservo Thessalis; tunc alitem factum ubi quaeram, videbo quando?"

23. (1) "At mihi scelus istud depellant caelites," inquam, "ut ego, quamvis ipsius aquilae sublimis volatibus toto caelo pervius, et supremi Iovis certus nuntius vel laetus armiger, tamen non ad meum nidulum post illam pinnarum dignitatem subinde devolem. (2) adiuro per dulcem istum capilli tui nodulum, quo meum vinxisti spiritum, me nullam aliam meae Fotidi malle. (3) tunc etiam istud meis cogitationibus occurrit: cum semel avem talem perunctus induero, domus omnis procul me vitare debere. quam pulchro enim quamque festivo matronae perfruentur amatore bubone? (4) quid, quod istas nocturnas aves, cum penetraverint larem quempiam, sollicite prehensas foribus videmus adfigi, ut, quod infaustis volatibus familiae minantur exitium, suis luant cruciatibus. (5) sed, quod sciscitari paene praeterivi, quo dicto factove, rursum—exutis pinnulis illis—ad meum redibo Lucium?"

(6) "Bono animo es, quod ad huius rei curam pertinet," ait. "nam mihi domina singula monstravit, quae possunt rursus in facies hominum tales figuras reformare. (7) nec istud factum putes ulla benivolentia, sed ut ei redeunti medela salubri possem subsistere. (8) specta denique, quam parvis quamque futtilibus tanta res procuretur herbulis: anethi modicum cum lauri foliis immissum rori fontano datur lavacrum et poculum."

24. (1) Haec identidem adseverans summa cum trepidatione inrepit cubiculum et pyxidem depromit arcula. (2) quam ego amplexus ac deosculatus prius, utque mihi prosperis faveret volatibus deprecatus, abiectis propere laciniis totis avide manus immersi et, haurito plusculo uncto, corporis mei membra perfricui. (3) iamque alternis conatibus libratis brachiis in avem similem gestiebam: nec ullae plumulae nec usquam pinnulae, (4) sed plane pili mei crassantur in setas, et cutis tenella duratur in corium, et in extimis palmulis perdito numero toti digiti coguntur in singulas ungulas, et de spinae meae termino grandis cauda procedit. (5) iam facies enormis et os prolixum et nares hiantes et labiae pendulae; sic et aures immodicis horripilant auctibus. (6) nec ullum miserae reformationis video solacium, nisi quod mihi—iam nequeunti tenere Fotidem—natura crescebat.

25. (1) Ac dum salutis inopia cuncta corporis mei considerans non avem me, sed asinum video, querens de facto Fotidis, sed iam humano gestu simul et voce privatus, quod solum poteram, postrema deiecta labia, umidis tamen oculis, oblicum respiciens ad illam tacitus expostulabam.

Metamorphoses III

(2) quae ubi primum me talem aspexit, percussit faciem suam manibus infestis et "Occisa sum misera," clamavit; "me trepidatio simul et festinatio fefellit et pyxidum similitudo decepit. (3) sed bene, quod facilior reformationis huius medela suppeditat. nam rosis tantum demorsicatis, exibis asinum, statimque in meum Lucium postliminio redibis. (4) atque utinam vesperi, de more, nobis parassem corollas aliquas, ne moram talem patereris vel noctis unius. sed primo diluculo remedium festinabitur tibi."

26. (1) Sic illa maerebat. Ego vero, quamquam perfectus asinus et pro Lucio iumentum, sensum tamen retinebam humanum. (2) diu denique ac multum mecum ipse deliberavi, an nequissimam facinerosissimamque illam feminam spissis calcibus feriens et mordicus adpetens necare deberem. (3) sed ab incepto temerario melior me sententia revocavit, ne, morte multata Fotide, salutares mihi suppetias rursus extinguerem. (4) deiecto itaque et quassanti capite, ac demussata temporali contumelia, durissimo casui meo serviens ad equum illum vectorem meum probissimum in stabulum concedo, ubi alium etiam Milonis quondam hospitis mei asinum stabulantem inveni. (5) atque ego rebar, si quod inesset mutis animalibus tacitum ac naturale sacramentum, agnitione ac miseratione quadam inductum, equum illum meum hospitium ac loca lautia mihi praebiturum. (6) sed pro Iuppiter hospitalis et Fidei secreta numina! praeclarus ille vector meus cum asino capita conferunt, in meamque perniciem ilico consentiunt (7) et verentes scilicet cibariis suis, vix me praesepio videre proximantem: deiectis auribus iam furentes infestis calcibus insecuntur. (8) et abigor quam procul ab ordeo, quod adposueram vesperi meis manibus illi gratissimo famulo.

27. (1) Sic adfectus atque in solitudinem relegatus, angulo stabuli concesseram. dumque de insolentia collegarum meorum mecum cogito, atque—in alterum diem auxilio rosario Lucius denuo futurus—equi perfidi vindictam meditor, (2) respicio (pilae mediae, quae stabuli trabes sustinebat, in ipso fere meditullio) Eponae deae simulacrum residens aediculae, quod accurate corollis roseis equidem recentibus fuerat ornatum. (3) denique, adgnito salutari praesidio, pronus spei, quantum extensis prioribus pedibus adniti poteram, insurgo valide et cervice prolixa nimiumque porrectis labiis, quanto maxime nisu poteram, corollas adpetebam. (4) quod me pessima scilicet sorte conantem, servulus meus (cui semper equi cura mandata fuerat) repente conspiciens, indignatus exsurgit (5) et "Quo usque tandem," inquit, "cantherium patiemur istum paulo ante cibariis iumentorum, nunc etiam simulacris deorum infestum? (6) quin iam ego istum sacrilegum debilem claudumque reddam." et statim telum aliquod quaeritans, temere fascem lignorum positum offendit, (7)

rimatusque frondosum fustem cunctis vastiorem, non prius miserum me tundere desiit, quam, sonitu vehementi et largo strepitu percussis ianuis, trepido etiam rumore viciniae, conclamatis latronibus, profugit territus.

28. (1) Nec mora, cum vi patefactis aedibus globus latronum invadit omnia, et singula domus membra cingit armata factio, et auxiliis hinc inde convolantibus obsistit discursus hostilis. (2) cuncti gladiis et facibus instructi noctem illuminant, coruscat in modum ortivi solis ignis et mucro. (3) tunc horreum quoddam satis validis claustris obseptum obseratumque (quod, mediis aedibus constitutum, gazis Milonis fuerat refertum) securibus validis adgressi diffindunt. (4) quo passim recluso totas opes vehunt, raptimque constrictis sarcinis singuli partiuntur. (5) sed gestaminum modus numerum gerulorum excedit. tunc opulentiae nimiae nimio ad extremas incitas deducti, nos duos asinos et equum meum productos e stabulo, (6) quantum potest, gravioribus sarcinis onerant, et—domo iam vacua—minantes baculis, exigunt, unoque de sociis ad speculandum (qui de facinoris inquisitione nuntiaret) relicto, nos crebra tundentes per avia montium ducunt concitos.

29. (1) Iamque rerum tantarum pondere et montis ardui vertice et prolixo satis itinere nihil a mortuo differebam. sed mihi sero quidem, serio tamen subvenit ad auxilium civile decurrere et interposito venerabili principis nomine tot aerumnis me liberare. (2) cum denique iam luce clarissima vicum quempiam frequentem et nundinis celebrem praeteriremus, inter ipsas turbelas Graecorum genuino sermone nomen augustum Caesaris invocare temptavi; (3) et "O" quidem tantum disertum et validum clamitavi, reliquum autem Caesaris nomen enuntiare non potui. (4) aspernati latrones clamorem absonum meum, caedentes hinc inde miserum corium nec cribris iam idoneum relinquunt. sed tandem mihi inopinatam salutem Iuppiter ille tribuit. (5) nam cum multas villulas et casas amplas praeterimus, hortulum quendam prospexi satis amoenum, in quo praeter ceteras gratas herbulas rosae virgines matutino rore florebant. (6) his inhians et spe salutis alacer ac laetus propius accessi, dumque iam labiis undantibus adfecto, consilium me subit longe salubrius, (7) ne, si rursum—asino remoto—prodirem in Lucium, evidens exitium inter manus latronum offenderem vel artis magicae suspectione, vel indicii futuri criminatione. (8) tunc igitur a rosis et quidem necessario temperavi et casum praesentem tolerans in asini faciem frena rodebam.

Commentary

1.1. **commodum ... et**: "it was just the time ... that." *commodum*: "a very short time before," or "at this very moment"; adverb.

punicantibus phaleris: "with crimson trappings." *phalerae, -arum,* f. pl. are the metal disks used to decorate a horse's harness. *punicans, -antis* means "inclining to red"; cf. the more common *puniceus, -a, -um,* "crimson." The reference is to the famous Homeric formula "When rosy-fingered dawn shone once more."

inequitabat < *inequitō, -āre,* "to ride into."

securae < *sēcūrus, -a, -um,* "free from care," "untroubled" (cf. OLD 1a).

revulsum < *revello, -vellere, -velli, -vulsum,* "to wrench off," "to tear away from" (normally + abl. of the thing from which one is torn); here used hyperbolically, + dative (OLD 3b).

1.2. **aestus**: *aestus, aestūs,* m. is literally "heat," but it can also mean "mental disturbance, anxiety, worry" (OLD 9b).

vesperni: If this reading of the MSS is accepted, *vespernus, -a, -um* must be a variant of *vespertinus, -a, -um,* "of or pertaining to the evening." At the end of *Met.* II, Lucius had apparently encountered three robbers on his way back from dinner with Byrrhena, and killed them.

complicitis < *complicō, -āre, -āvī* or *-uī, -ātum* or *-itum,* "to fold together, "tie up"; here "to fold up the limbs" (OLD 3b).

in alternas digitorum vicissitudines: i.e. Lucius' hands were clasped together and his fingers were interlocked.

grabatum < *grabatus* (or *grabattus*) *-i,* m., "a low bed; a cot, a camp-bed."

cossim: "squatting," "on the haunches"; adverb.

forum ... iudicia ... sententiam ... carnificem: Lucius is thinking of the stages of a criminal trial: after being brought into the forum defendants would undergo trials (*iudicia*); a trial would result in a formal judgement (*sententia*), and a guilty verdict would send a defendant to the executioner (*carnifex*).

imaginabundus: *imāginābundus, -a, -um,* "picturing to oneself."

1.3. **obtinget** < *obtingō, -ere, -gī,* "fall to one's lot," "happen to" (+ dat.).

trinae caedis = *triplicis caedis.*

perlitum < *perlinō, perlinere, (perlēvī), perlitum,* "to smear all over with."

delibutum < *dēlibūtus, -a, -um,* "thickly smeared."

1.4. **fore** = *futūrum esse,* cf. AG §170a.

Chaldaeus Diophanes: At *Met.* II.12 we learned that this fortune-teller had predicted both that Lucius would become famous, and that he would be the subject of a long book.

obstinate: because Diophanes had persisted in his prophecy of Lucius' fame: *multa respondit et oppido mira et satis varia (Met. 2.12).*

1.5. **identidem**: "repeatedly"; adverb.

replicans < *replicō, -āre, (-āvī), -ātum,* "to fold back"; "to go over something (in the mind) again and again" (OLD 3).

heiulabam < *eiulō (heiulō), -āre,* "to shout heia," i.e. to shout a cry of anguish; also transitive, "to bewail something."

quati < *quatiō, -tere, -ssum,* "to shake"; historical infinitive, cf. AG §463.

interdum: "At times, sometimes" is the classical meaning of this word, but it can also mean, as here, "meanwhile" (OLD 2).

perstrepi < *perstrepō, -ere,* "to make a loud noise," also transitive, "to make something resound with a loud noise"; historical infinitive.

2.1. **nec mora, cum**: literally "there was no delay, when ..."; i.e. "all at once."

magistratibus eorumque ministris: These ablatives depend on *cuncta completa (sunt).*

et turbae miscellaneae: best understood as genitive, also dependent on *completa*; this change of case, with an ablative and genitive both dependent on the same word, is not common, but there are good parallels in Sallust. Some editors supply a word in the ablative, e.g. *turbae miscellaneae <coetu> cuncta completa.*

statimque: For the use of *-que* for "beginning a sentence, introducing a fresh event or situation, a further point in an argument, etc." see OLD 4.

lictores duo: Lictors (there is no other English word) were the attendants of a Roman magistrate, who carried the rods (and sometimes axes) symbolic of magisterial authority.

immissa manu: "making an arrest." The technical term for making an arrest is *manum inicere* (used below at 3.10.3); *manum immittere* is perhaps an intentionally untechnical variation.

occipiunt < *occipiō, -ipere, -ēpī, -eptum,* "to engage in (an occupation)"; "to begin."

2.2. **primum angiportum:** "the first street"; *angiportum, -ī,* n. or *angiportus, -ūs,* m. means "narrow passage, lane."

insistimus < *insistō, -ere, institī;* the basic meaning is "to stand on," hence *viam insistere* means "to set out on a road" (OLD 1.b).

in populum effusa: "having poured forth in a crowd" (literally "having poured forth *into* a crowd").

2.3. **quamquam ... incederem:** *quamquam* can take not only the indicative but also the subjunctive (OLD 2).
inferos < *inferus, -a, -um,* "lower"; as nom. pl. substantive = "the dead" or "the gods of the underworld."
obliquato ... aspectu: "out of the corner of my eye."
admirationis maximae: genitive of quality, cf. AG §345.

2.4. **circumsedentis:** As we soon learn, the people were seated at their places at the forum. It follows that the following sentence (*tandem ... adstituor*) is a flashback, though *tandem* does not seem the obvious way to make this clear.

nemo prorsum: *prorsum* (or *prorsus,* the more common form) is an adverb that intensifies the preceding word: "absolutely no one."

qui non risu dirumperetur: relative clause of characteristic, cf. AG §535a.

2.5. **plateis** < *platea, -ae,* f., "avenue" (a street wider than than an *angiportum*).

lustralibus piamentis: ablative of means, i.e. "by ritual purification ceremonies."

minas portentorum: "the threats presented by portents"; *portentorum* is an appositional genitive, cf. AG §343d.

hostiis circumforaneis: "by means of sacrificial animals led round the forum." The best known example of this ritual use of animals was the annual purification ceremony at Rome, the Ambarvalia.

expiant < *expiō, -āre, -āvī, -ātum,* "to atone; to purify"; also "to avert divine disfavor by means of expiatory rites" (OLD 4).

angulatim: "into every nook and cranny" (with *circumductus*); adverb.

forum eiusque tribunal: The forum was the marketplace; it would typically have a raised platform at one end, the tribunal, where legal proceedings were conducted.

adstituor < *astituō (adstituō), -uere, -uī, -ūtum,* "to make to stand before, to place near."

2.6. **suggestu** < *suggestus, -ūs*, m., "platform," i.e. the tribunal just mentioned.

propter coetus multitudinem: *coetus, -ūs*, m., here "crowd, assembly."

pressurae: probably depends on *periclitaretur*, i.e. "was in danger of getting squeezed."

iudicium tantum: "a trial of such magnitude" (< *tantus, -a, -um*).

theatro: ablative of place where.

redderetur: depends on *flagitant*; on the omission of *ut* with verbs of commanding cf. AG §565a. *iudicium reddere* means "to grant a trial" (OLD *reddo* 14b).

2.7. **caveae conseptum**: "the enclosure of the *cavea*"; *consaeptum (conseptum), -ī*, n., means "enclosure," and the *cavea* was the semicircular area in which the theater audience sat.

2.8. **fartim**: "tightly"; "like stuffing or mincemeat"; adverb.

stipaverant < *stīpō, stīpāre, stīpāvī, stīpātum*, "to compress, to crowd."

lacunaria: here perhaps simply "holes." *lacūnar, -āris*, n., means "ceiling panel," particularly in a coffered ceiling; it is hard to imagine that anyone could sit in one, so perhaps Apuleius imagines that people are peeping through holes in the roof, seen from below as holes in the ceiling panels.

pericula salutis = *pericula vitae*.

2.9. **proscaenium medium**: "the middle of the stage."

velut quandam victimam: *victima* has here its technical religious sense of "sacrificial victim."

publica ministeria = *publici ministri* (cf. OLD *ministerium* 5).

orchestrae mediae: dative with a verb of motion (this construction is found only in poetry or in post-classical prose, cf. AG §428h). The orchestra was the area in front of the stage, assigned to the most prominent members of the audience.

3.1. **sic**: here "this having been done" (cf. OLD 9a).

boatu < *boātus, -ūs*, m., "shouting" (rare).

ad dicendi spatium: "to regulate the time for speaking"; literally "with a view to achieving a (fixed) amount of time for speaking," cf. OLD *ad* 45.

vasculo quodam = *vasculo cuidam*, with *infusa aqua*; Apuleius writes *aliquo* for *alicui*, and *quovis* for *cuivis*. *vasculus* is the diminutive of *vas*. The reference here is to the waterclock (clepsydra), used to measure the time taken by speakers in court.

in vicem: "like" (+ gen.). *vicis, vicis,* f., means "a turn"; *ad vicem* + gen. means "after the manner of" (OLD 9b), and Apuleius uses *in vicem* in the same way.

coli < *cōlum, -i,* n., "strainer, sieve."

graciliter: "thinly," i.e. "with small holes"; adverb.

fistulato < *fistulātus, -a, -um,* "fitted with pipes (*fistulae*)," i.e. "perforated."

per hoc: "because of this," i.e. "because it was perforated."

guttatim: "drop by drop"; adverb.

defluo < *defluus, -a, -um,* "flowing down"; (of a container) "emitting a flow."

infusa aqua: ablative absolute.

3.2. **Neque ... ac:** "While not ... (yet) at the same time" (cf. OLD *neque* 8a). The ponderous opening is typical of a courtroom speech.

exemplo serio: "by a stern precedent"; ablative of means.

profutura < *prōsum, prōdesse, prōfuī,* "be useful."

Quirites: The archaic name for Roman citizens is regularly used in speeches addressed to the Roman people; its use by a local magistrate in a Greek city is striking.

3.3. **congruit** < *congruō, -ere, -uī,* "to be fitting," here used impersonally (cf. OLD 3).

lanienam < *laniēna, -ae,* f., "a butcher's shop"; "butchery."

commisserit = *commiserit.* < *committō, committere, comīsī, comissum,* here "commit, perpetrate" (cf. OLD 17).

3.4. **nec ... putetis** = *nolite putare*; cf. AG §440 with note 3. It was a commonplace of rhetoric for the speaker to deny any personal involvement in the matter at hand.

in hodiernum: "until today," i.e. "up to today."

pervigilem < *pervigil, -ilis,* "wakeful, "night-long"; construe with *diligentiam*.

3.5. **denique:** The basic meaning of *denique* is "finally, at last," but it can also have the weaker senses of "in short, to sum up" (cf. OLD 3) or "in point of fact, indeed" (cf. OLD 5).

fere iam tertia vigilia: "about the time of the third watch."

ostiatim: "from door to door"; adverb.

3.6. **conspicio**: historical present (cf. AG §469); the historical present often takes secondary sequence, cf. AG §485c.

istum: prosecution speeches regularly use *iste, ista, istud* as a contemptuous way of referring to the defendant, cf. OLD B.5b.

operantem: "busy with" (+ dat.).

spirantes adhuc, corporibus in multo sanguine palpitantes: If the MSS text is right, *corporibus* is presumably an ablative of respect, cf. AG §418; scholars have suggested instead *spirantibus adhuc corporibus, in multo sanguine palpitantes*. < *palpitō, -āre, -āvī,* "to beat, to pulsate."

3.7. **perpetem noctem** < *perpes, perpetis*, adj., "continuous"; accusative of extent of time.

delituit < *dēlitiscō, -iscere, -uī*, "to hide oneself."

3.8. **deum**: *deum* is a common alternative form for *deōrum*.

priusquam iste ... elaberetur: "before this (culprit) could slip away." *priusquam* with the subjunctive indicates the relationship is not purely temporal, but that there is an element of purpose or anticipation (cf. OLD 2a; AG §§550-551).

mane: "the morning," object of *praestolatus*; *mane* is not only an adverb ("in the morning") but also an indeclinable neuter noun, cf. OLD 3.

praestolatus < *praestōlor, -ārī, -ātus*, "wait for, expect."

sacramentum < *sacrāmentum, -ī*, n., "oath" but also, as here, "obligation" (OLD 3).

3.9. **reum ... reum ... reum**: Note the anaphora, (repetition of the same word) and the tricolon decrescendo (three phrases, with each successive phrase weaker than the preceding one): the speaker's climactic emphasis on the fact that Lucius is from out of town is supposed to strike us as incongruous.

constanter: "firmly, without ado" (OLD 3b); adverb.

quod etiam ... vindicaretis: i.e. "which you would punish severely even if the culprit were a citizen"; relative clause of characteristic, cf. AG §534-535. Apuleius can use *vindico* to mean "punish a crime," with *in* + accusative indicating the person from whom the punishment is to be exacted (cf. OLD 5a).

4.2. **tunc temporis**: "at that moment"; for the partitive genitive with adverbs see AG §346.3; the pleonasm is characteristic of Apuleius' non-classical style.

hercules: an interjection; more formal Latin would be *me hercule*.

intuens < *intueor, intuērī, intuitus,* "look at," but here "reflect on, consider" (cf. OLD 6).

oborta divinitus audacia: "with a boldness sent by heaven." < *oborior, -īrī, -tus,* "spring up"; *dīvīnitus* is an adverb, "by divine inspiration." *audacia* is used regularly in a good sense, cf. OLD 1a.

sic ad illa: sc. *inquam.*

4.3. **quam:** with *arduum.*

trinis = *tribus.*

arguatur < *arguō, -uere, -uī, -ūtum,* here "to accuse someone of something," with the accusation in the genitive, cf. OLD 4b.

de facto confiteatur ultro: not "admits that he did the deed" (van der Paardt), but "freely reveals the truth about the deed"; if Lucius were actually to confess, he could hardly hope to persuade his judges of his innocence.

4.4. **quod sit innocens:** *quod* can be used with the subjunctive (or indicative) to introduce an indirect statement, though the usage is rare and unclassical; cf. OLD 5.

publica: "generally available" cf. OLD *publicus* 4.

discrimen capitis: "life-threatening danger"; *caput, capitis,* n., can mean the "life" of a person, especially one in danger, cf. OLD 4a.

merito: "fault" cf. OLD *meritum* 3b.

rationabilis indignationis eventu fortuito: "by the chance outcome of a justifiable anger." Lucius' defense is that the deaths were (a) not intentional and (b) a consequence of his justifiable anger at seeing what he thought were robbers.

invidiam: parallel to *discrimen,* i.e. direct object of *sustinere.*

frustra: "mistakenly" cf. OLD 2.

sustinere < *sustineō, sustinēre, sustinuī,* here "bear the weight of" (cf. OLD 5a).

5.1. **serius:** comparative of the adverb *sērō,* "late."

reciperem: *recipio* with a reflexive pronoun as direct object means "withdraw, return" (cf. OLD 12a).

potulentus: "drunk" (OLD 1).

alioquin: *aliōquīn* usually means "otherwise," but Apuleius uses it to mean "as a matter of fact"; cf. OLD 4.

diffitebor < *diffiteor, -ērī,* "to disavow, deny." The use of the future here is not strictly accurate, but is a colloquialism found also in English.

Apuleius, *Metamorphoses* III

hospitii < *hospitium, -iī*, n., "hospitality," but also "guest accomodation" or "lodgings" (cf. OLD 3).

autem: The basic sense of *autem* is of course adversative ("but, however") but it can also be used to introduce an explanation (cf. OLD 4).

devorto: an alternate form of *dēvertō, -tere, -tī, -sum*, "to turn aside", "to make a detour" and thus "to (turn off the road and) stay with someone."

5.2. **aditum temptantes**: The reader of Book II realizes at this point that Lucius is lying about the details of the supposed attack.

5.3. **et ceteros**: *et* is almost untranslatable; the robber was inciting the others as well as himself.

5.4. **quam**: exclamatory, with *maribus* and *alacribus*; cf. OLD 2.

maribus < *mās, maris*, adj., "male," here "manly."

facessat < *facessō, -ere, -īvī* or *iī, -ītum* means not only "perform; accuse" but also "go away, depart" (so also below at 3.10.1).

caedes ambulet: hortatory subjunctive; the robber supposedly used a striking personification.

5.5. **feriatur** < *feriō, ferīre*, "strike" but also "kill" (cf. OLD 3a).

sic: "thus"; correlative with *si*, as often. See AG §512b.

recedemus ... si ... reliquerimus: future more vivid condition; cf. AG §514 B 1b for protasis with future perfect indicative.

5.6. **extremos**: *extremus* can mean "desperate, stopping at nothing" (cf. OLD 4b and 4c).

eximie: "exceptionally"; adverb.

5.7. **gladiolo**: Note the diminutive, which is perhaps inherently funny; by stressing that it was only a little sword Lucius tries to make himself look less like a brutal murderer.

proterrere < *prōterreō, -ere, uī, -itum*, "to frighten off."

adgressus sum < *aggredior (adgredior), aggredī, aggressus*, normally "advance," but here "attempt, begin" to do something, with infinitives.

5.8. **illi barbari prorsus**: "those absolute barbarians" (for *prorsus* see on 3.2.4 above).

neque ... et: "while not ... (yet) at the same time"; cf. OLD 8a. *neque ... et* is more common than *neque ... ac*, used above at 3.3.2.

capessunt < *capessō, capessere, capessīvī* (or *-iī*), *-ītum*, "to take hold of, grasp," here "take to" (cf. OLD 7).

cum me viderent: The *cum* clause is in secondary sequence because the main verb *resistunt* is historical present; cf. AG §485e.

in ferro: "armed with a sword"; this use of *in* with the ablative, instead of the ordinary ablative of means or instrument, is post-classical.

6.1. **dirigitur**: *aciem dirigere* is a technical term for drawing up battle lines.

dux et signifer: "the leader and standard-bearer"; a pompous expression for "leader."

ceterorum: *cēterus, -a, -um* in the plural can be used as a substantive ("the rest, the others"), cf. OLD 2a; here the meaning seems little different from *eorum*.

viribus: *vīs, vis*, f., in the plural can mean "hostile strength, force," cf. OLD 21.

illico: "on the spot"; "at once"; adverb.

reflexum < *reflectō, reflectere, reflexī, reflexum*, "bend back."

effligere < *efflīgō, efflīgere, efflīxī, efflīctum*, "strike dead, kill."

6.2. **quem**: The antecedent is *lapide*, in the previous sentence.

porrigi < *porrigō, porrigere, porrexī, porrectum*, "stretch out," but also "hold out" (for someone to take), cf. OLD 6a; notice the passive.

flagitat: The subject of the relative clause (not the sentence as a whole) is *dux et signifer* in the previous sentence.

prosterno < *prosternō, prosternere, prostrāvī, prostrātum*, "knock over, lay low."

pedibus meis: construe with *inhaerentem*.

mordicus: "with the teeth, by biting"; adverb.

temperato: almost "skillful" or "well-aimed"; *tempero* can mean "to control" (physically), cf. OLD 8.

offenso < *offendō, -dere, -dī, -sum*, "to bump into," thus "to strike" (cf. OLD 1d).

peremo: alternate form of *perimō, -imere, -ēmī, -emptum*, "destroy, kill."

6.3. **domoque ... protecta**: ablative absolute. For the declension of *domus, -ūs*, f. cf. AG §93.

impunem = *impunitum*.

tantillo < *tantillus, -a, -um*, "so small."

crimine postulatus: *crimine postulare (aliquem)* means "to prosecute" someone; literally "to demand someone's appearance by means of a charge."

probe = *bene*.

commodis < *commodum, -ī,* n., "advantage, convenience."

6.4. **reatum** < *reātus, -ūs,* m., "accusation" (+ genitive).

6.5. **vel ... ac** = "either ... or," cf. OLD *vel* 2a.

ne omnino = *ne omnino quidem,* i.e. "not even in any circumstances," cf. OLD *omnino* 3a. For *ne* = *ne ... quidem* see OLD *ne* 7.

vel certe: "or, if you prefer, at least ..."; *vel* can introduce a command, indicating that what is being suggested is one available option, cf. OLD 1a. For *certe* meaning "at least, at any rate," cf. OLD 2a.

monstretur: hortatory subjunctive.

flagitium ... admissum: *flagitium admittere* means "to commit a crime."

7.1. **profatus** < *profor, profārī, profātus,* "to speak out, to tell."

per ... per: For the use of *per* in forms of entreaty see OLD 10b; *per deos immortalis* (Sallust, *Bellum Catilinae* 51) = "by the immortal gods."

pignorum < *pignus, -eris* or *-oris,* n., "a pledge," but also "a child" (because a child was seen as guarantee of a marriage). The genitive here is objective: "love of their children" (cf. AG §348).

deprecabar < *dēprecor, dēprecārī, dēprecātus,* here "entreat" (cf. OLD 3).

7.2. **fletuum:** objective genitive, i.e. "pity for my tears" (cf. AG §348).

omnis = *omnēs*.

Solis et Iustitiae: The Greek goddess Themis (= Iustitia) was said to be the daughter of the Sun.

oculos: Since the eyes are particularly important in witnessing, they are regularly invoked in oaths; cf. OLD *oculus* 1d.

7.3. **aspectu relato:** i.e. "lifting up my face."

prorsus: construe with *totum populum,* i.e. "absolutely the entire population."

risu cachinnabili diffluebant: a parenthesis. *cachinnābilis, -e,* a word that occurs only here, is not redundant with *risu,* but shows that the laughter was "boisterous" (OLD), or perhaps even "scornful" (van der Paardt).

secus: "differently"; adverb.

parentemque meum: *parens, -ntis*, m., literally means "parent," and thus "relative," but the word can be used in an honorific way for an older friend.

dissolutum < *dissoluō, -uere, -uī, -ūtum*, "to break up." It is tempting to translate *dissolutum* here as "broken up" (with laughter), but OLD 6 understands the verb here as "to deprive of strength, weaken, wear out."

7.4. **en:** *ēn*, interjection, "Observe!" (often ironic).

reus capitis: "a defendant on a capital charge," cf. OLD *caput* 5.

inducor < *indūcō, -cere, -xī, -ctum*, here "to bring someone in as a defendant," OLD 1b.

contentus, quod: "content with the fact that"; *contentus* can govern a clause introduced by *eo quod*, or by *quod* alone.

nec = *ne ... quidem*, like *ne* in 3.6.5.

adsistendi solacium < *assistō, -ere, astitī*, "to stand near"; the word also has the technical meaning of "support someone in court," cf. OLD 3c. For the gerund as an objective genitive cf. AG §504.

perhibuit < *perhibeō, perhibēre, perhibuī, perhibitum*, here in its original meaning of "present, bestow."

cachinnat < *cachinnō, -āre, -āvī, -ātum*, usually "to laugh" (intransitive), but here "laugh at" (OLD 2).

8.1. **lacrimosa et flebilis:** almost redundant, but *lacrimosus* emphasizes the actual tears, while *flebilis* also refers to the sorrow behind them.

pone: preposition + acc., "behind."

anus alia: *anus, -ūs*, f., "old woman." Since the woman with the baby was presumably a young mother, *alia* here is presumably in apposition to *anus*: "another woman—an old one."

pannis < *pannus, -ī*, also *pannum, ī*, n., "piece of cloth, rag." Litigants in Roman courts routinely dressed in rags to excite the sympathy of their judges.

obsita < *obsitus, -a, -um*, "covered in, enveloped in."

oleagineos < *oleāgineus, -a, -um*, "of the olive tree." The olive branch symbolized peace rather than compassion, but olive branches were used in supplication.

utraeque < *uterque, utraque, utrumque*, originally "which of two" (interrogative or indefinite), but the plural is used in colloquial Latin to mean "both."

8.2. **circumfusae:** "surrounding"; *circumfundō, -fundere, -fūdī*,

-*fūsum* means literally "to pour around"; also, in the passive, "to be situated around" (cf. OLD 4).

se lugubriter eiulantes: *ēiulō, -āre*, "to shriek"; "to bewail" (here with reflexive pronoun as direct object, OLD b). *lūgubriter*, "sorrowfully"; adverb (rare).

8.3. **Per commune ius humanitatis**: *humanitas* here means "mankind." For the use of *per* in entreaties see on 3.7.1.

miseremini: imperative < *misereor, -ērī, -itus*, "have pity on" (+ genitive).

viduitati ac solitudini: The young mother is a widow, and the old woman was presumably a mother.

de vindicta < *vindicta, -ae*, f., here "vengeance, punishment." The use of *de* to indicate cause or instrument is postclassical, cf. OLD 14.

8.4. **destituti** < *destituō, destituere, destituī, destitūtum*, here "to abandon" (OLD 3a).

de latronis huius sanguine: "with this brigand's blood"; for *de* + abl. indicating the source of something cf. OLD 7.

litate < *litō, -āre, -āvī, -ātum*, "to propitiate" (+ dative).

8.5. **qui maior natu**: sc. *erat*. For *natū* as one of the few common supines in -*ū*, cf. AG §510. We now learn that the presiding magistrates were two in number (Italian towns were typically governed by *duoviri*), and that the older one was also the magistrate in charge of the case.

ad populum talia: sc. *dixit*.

serio: "seriously"; adverb.

nec = *ne ... quidem*, as at 3.7.4.

diffiteri < *diffiteor, diffitērī*, "disavow, deny."

subsiciva < *subsicīvus, -a, -um*, "left over."

ut ... requiramus: for substantive clauses of result with verbs indicating the accomplishment of an effort (*reliquum est* etc.) cf. AG §568.

8.6. **nec ... veri simile est**: "it is not likely that," introducing an indirect statement; for *veri similis*, literally "apparently consistent with the truth," cf. OLD *vērus* 7b.

evitasse < *ēvītō, -āre, -āvī, -ātum*, "to kill"; a rare and archaic word, not to be confused with its more common homonym, which means "shun, avoid."

prohinc: "therefore, hence"; adverb.

tormentis < *tormentum, -ī,* n., here "torture." Slaves were regularly tortured in Roman criminal proceedings, but in theory citizens were exempt; part of the horror of Lucius' predicament is that the town of Hypata seems to be a law unto itself.

8.7. **et qui comitabatur eum puer** = *puer qui eum comitabitur*; *puer* here = "slave, servant."

clanculo: "secretly"; adverb (a rare alternative for *clam*).

per quaestionem < *quaestiō, -ōnis,* f., "investigation; examination of witnesses." In a legal context the word often implies, as here, that the examination will be conducted under torture.

tam dirae factionis < *factiō, -ōnis,* f., "faction, party of conspirators" (cf. OLD 4a); the word has a quasi-political sense, since the magistrate is overdramatizing the nature of Lucius' supposed gang.

funditus: "from the roots, from the ground," i.e. "utterly"; adverb.

perematur < *perīmō (peremō), perimere, perēmī, peremptum,* "to destroy."

9.1. **cum ... cum**: anaphora (cf. on 3.3.9) and asyndeton (the omission of a connective to indicate intense emotion). The *cum* clauses here are examples of *cum inversum*: the indication of time is placed in the main clause, and the principal actions are placed in the two subordinate clauses; cf. AG §546a.

ritu Graeciensi ignis et rota: the wheel (on which victims were turned) was, combined with fire, a characteristically Greek form of torture. *ritu* + genitive means "in the manner of."

flagrorum < *flagrum, -ī,* n., "whip."

9.2. **oppido**: "very much, utterly"; adverb. The word is archaic, but quite common in Apuleius.

quod ... licuerit: see on 3.4.4. for *quod* + subjunctive to indicate indirect statement.

integro: supply *corpore*; the Greeks and Romans thought it particularly important for corpses to buried intact; at *Met.* 2.22 the corpse is guarded to prevent mutilation.

saltim: a variant of *saltem*, "at least"; adverb.

9.3. **Prius ... quam** = *priusquam,* conj., "before," which can be written as two separated words.

peremptorem < *peremptor, -ōris,* m., "killer" (rare).

9.4. **arrecti** < *arrigō, -igere, -exī, -ectum,* "to stand; to arouse."

pro modo: "in proportion to" (+ genitive); cf. OLD *modus* 3b.

Apuleius, *Metamorphoses* III

saeviatis < *saeviō, saevīre, saevīi, saevītum*, "to rage, to act savagely."

9.5. **adplauditur** < *applaudō (adplaudō), -dere, -sī, -sum*, "to strike; to applaud"; here used impersonally, OLD 2.

9.6. **luctantem** < *luctor, -arī, -atum*, "to wrestle with, to struggle."

rennuentem < *renuō (rennuō), renuere, renuī*, "to refuse, to decline."

instaurare < *instaurō, -āre, -āvī, -ātum*, "to repeat."

ostensione < *ostensiō, -ōnis*, f., "display" (rare).

manum denique ipsam e regione lateris tundentes: The lictors begin by pushing Lucius' reluctant hand up from where it is hanging down by his side; *tundentes* is a vivid and dramatic word here, meaning that they pushed his hand by assailing it with blows.

in exitium suum: The lictors' pushing of his hand will result, Lucius thinks, in the destruction of that hand (and all the rest of him), since it is about to remove the shroud covering the three corpses.

9.7. **ingratis**: "unwillingly"; adverb.

licet: here with virtually the sense of a conjunction meaning "although" (OLD 4c).

retexi < *retegō, -ere, -xī, -ctum*, "to uncover." The tense has shifted from the historical present (*succumbo*) to the perfect.

quae facies rei?: *facies* here means "appearance" (of things); OLD 3.

9.8. **in peculio Proserpinae**: "among the possessions of Proserpina." *Peculium* is a technical term for the personal possessions of a slave or a family member subject to the *patria potestas* of a *paterfamilias*; technically such persons could own no property of their own, but they were allowed control over an unofficial property called a *peculium*.

Orci familia: Orcus (= Pluto) was king of Hades. A Roman's *familia* included not only relatives but also slaves.

in contrariam faciem obstupefactus: "astounded at the completely different appearance of things." With the accusative *in* can mean "in reference to, respecting, with regard to," cf. OLD 17a.

haesi < *haereō, haerēre, haesī, haesum*, "to stick," but also "to stop dead, freeze" (cf. OLD 10).

expedire < *expediō, -īre, -īvī* or *-iī, -ītum*, here "explain" (cf. OLD 4).

9.9. **iugulatorum** < *iugulō, -āre, -āvī, -ātum*, "to kill, to slaughter."

utres < *uter, utris*, m. (or n.), "a (leather) bag," i.e. a wineskin.

secti < *secō, -āre, -uī, -tum*, "to cut; cut into pieces."

foraminibus < *forāmen, -inis*, n., "a hole."

10.1. **ille quorundam astu paulisper cohibitus risus**: i.e. the laughter which *some* people managed, cunningly, to restrain for a little while. < *astus, -ūs*, m., "cunning, craft, guile"; ablative of means.

exarsit in plebem < *exardescō, -ere, -arsī, -arsum*, "catch fire, break out," here "break out among (lit. "onto) the people" (OLD 4.d).

gratulari < *grātulor, -ārī, -ātus*, "give thanks" (+ dative); historical infinitive, cf. AG §463. Many editors accept the emendation *graculari*, i.e. "they cawed like jackdaws."

sedare: historical infinitive.

et certe: *certe* here means "at least"; cf. OLD 2a.

delibuti < *dēlibūtus, -a, -um*, here "deeply imbued (with a feeling)" (OLD b).

theatro: In poetry and later prose the ablative without a preposition can indicate place from which, cf. AG §428f.

facessunt < *facessō, -ere, -īvī* or *iī, -ītum*, here "go away, depart, as at 3.5.4.

10.2. **laciniam** < *lacinia, -ae*, f., normally "fringe, hem," but here "coverlet" (referring to the *pallium* that had covered the three "corpses").

fixus in lapidem: "turned into stone."

una de ceteris ... statuis: "one of the other statues"; *ūnus, -a, -um* usually means "one in particular," but it can also mean "a certain one", cf. OLD 11; this usage approaches that of an indefinite article (cf. Italian *un, una*, French *un, une*), as in Petronius 26.8: *unus servus Agamemnonis*.

10.3. **prius ... quam**: See on 3.9.3.

ab inferis emersi: "I emerged from (the land of) the dead"; a proverbial expression for "I returned to life."

Milon hospes: Milo was Lucius' host (*hospes*) in Hypata.

iniecta manu: *manum inicere* is a legal term, referring to the formal assertion of ownership in court.

promicantibus < *prōmicō, -āre*, "to start forward, to shoot out" (rare, but also at 3.21.5).

crebra: "frequently, repeatedly"; *crēber, -bra, -brum* means "densely packed, frequent," and the neuter plural is used as an adverb (strictly speaking a cognate accusative, cf. AG §390b).

singultientem < *singultiō, -īre*, "gasp, sob."

clementi violentia: oxymoron.

10.4. **amfractus:** an alternative spelling of *anfractus, -ūs*, m., "a bend," thus "a bend in the road, a detour" (OLD 3c).

solatur: Notice that the tense has shifted from the perfect (*perduxit*) to the historical present.

10.5. **indignationem iniuriae:** *iniuriae* is an objective genitive (cf. AG §348), though here the sense is virtually causal.

altius: The comparative form of the Latin adjective can be used not only as a true comparative ("he is bigger than I am") but also as a kind of ironic positive ("he is rather big"); cf. AG §291.

11.1. **monitis** < *monita, -ōrum*, n. pl., "warnings, praecepts."

gestiunt < *gestiō, gestīre, gestīvī* or *gestiī*, "be eager to, want."

prosapiae < *prosapia, -ae*, f., "lineage, family" (rare).

vestrae familiae nobilitas: At the very beginning of the novel (*Met.* 1.2) we learn that Lucius is related on his mother's side to Plutarch.

conplectitur < *complector (conplector), complectī, complexus*, "to embrace"; here in the figurative sense of "extend over, spread over" (OLD 6c).

11.2. **ne** = *ne ... quidem*, as at 3.6.5.

contumeliae causa < *contumēlia, -ae*, f., "insult"; *causa* is ablative ("on account of"), cf. AG §359b.

perpessus es < *perpetior, perpetī, perpessus*, "undergo, experience."

angorem < *angor, -ōris*, m., here "anguish, anxiety."

11.3. **lusus** < *lusus, -ūs*, m., "game," but here "joke, prank" (cf. OLD 3).

deo Risui: The notion that a god named "Laughter" should be celebrated in this way is apparently an invention of Apuleius, though the god himself is not; Plutarch mentions a cult of Γέλως (Laughter) at Sparta, of all places.

reverticula < *reverticulum, -ī*, n., "the coming round again" (of heavenly bodies, or events).

commenti novitate: "because of the novelty of the trick." < *commentum, -ī*, n., "scheme; invention."

florescit < *flōrescō, -ere*, "to flower; to grow" but here "to increase in renown, prosperity etc." (OLD 3).

11.4. **ex animo:** "sincerely," cf. OLD *animus* 8.

laetabit < *laetō, -āre, āvī, -ātum*, "gladden, cheer."

11.5. **pro ista gratia:** "in return for your wonderful kindness"; for this meaning of *pro* + ablative cf. OLD 10.

patronum scribsit: sc. *te*.

in aere: *aes, aeris*, n., means "bronze"; *in* + the ablative here expresses the material used (OLD *in* 44b).

imago tua: Statues were in fact erected to Apuleius himself: Apul. *Flor.* 16; Aug. *Epist.* 138.

11.6. **splendidissima ... civitas:** vocative, in apposition to *tibi*.

honorum talium parem gratiam memini: "I record a gratitude equal to such honors." In classical Latin we would expect *par* to be construed with a dative. For *gratiam memini*, "record one's gratitude," cf. OLD *meminī* 5b.

verum: "but" (the regular meaning).

dignioribus meique maioribus: *mei* is genitive of comparison; this use of the genitive is not found in classical Latin, which uses the ablative instead.

12.1. **pudenter:** "with a sense for what is proper, modestly"; adverb.

renidens < *renīdeō, -ēre*, "to shine, reflect; smile back at, beam."

refingens < *refingō, -ere*, "to refashion, reshape"; here possibly "pretend."

12.2. **famulus** < *famulus, -ī*, m., "servant, slave."

parens: here "relative, kinswoman."

Byrrhena: Lucius' kinswoman, who had invited him to dinner on the night of his attack on the "three robbers."

convivii < *convīvium, -iī*, n., "dinner party."

sero: "late, tardily, at a late hour"; adverb. Here what the slave means is "yesterday evening."

desponderas < *despondeō, -dēre, -dī, -sum*, "to promise (oneself)." At dinner the night before Byrrhena had invited Lucius to help in the celebration of Risus that was to take place the next day (2.31). At the time this sounded like a simple invitation to the feast, but Byrrhena's words subsequently turned out to be an ironic reference to the joke played on Lucius. Now, however, she reverts to the non-ironic meaning of her words, and insists that the invitation had been given and accepted.

admonet < *admoneō, -ēre, -uī, -itum*, "to remind (someone) of something" (+ genitive), cf. OLD 1b.

12.3. **Quam vellem:** Exclamatory *quam* can modify verbs, cf. OLD 2.

parens: vocative. It is odd that Lucius seems to be addressing Byrrhena directly, since he is merely replying to an invitation delivered by her servant. This may be an example of Apuleius' carelessness about details, but it is also possible that Lucius is simply dictating his reply.

per fidem: often an exclamation, "by my faith!," but here apparently the equivalent of *ex fide*, "in good faith" (cf. OLD 6c). Lucius cannot accept the invitation due to a prior engagement.

12.4. **per hodierni diei praesentissimum numen adiurans:** i.e. Milo invoked the god Risus.

eius: we would expect *suae*, but later authors can use *is, ea, id* instead of the indirect reflexive, cf. AG §300.2b.

pignerarer < *pignerō, -āre, -āvī, -ātum*, "give as a pledge" hence "bind oneself to, make an engagement for" (OLD 2a), apparently with the dative.

discedit ... patitur: historical present.

prohinc: "therefore, hence"; adverb.

epulare vadimonium < *epulāris, -e*, "of a banquet."
< *vadimōnium, -(i)ī*, n., "pledge, surety," the legal term for a guarantee that a defendant will appear in court (like our bail, except that the *vadimonium* is posted by a third party). The expression *epulare vadimonium* is thus a joke, e.g. "gastronomic guarantee."

12.5. **iussis balnearibus adsequi** < *balnearia, -ium*, n. pl., "bath utensils; bathing supplies"; ordering utensils "to follow" is apparently the equivalent of ordering someone to bring them.

adambulabam < *adambulō, -āre*, "to walk near, walk beside" (+ dative).

obtectus < *obtego, -tegere, -texī, -tectum*, "to cover" or "hide."

12.6. **qui laverim, qui terserim, qui domum rursum reverterim:** *qui* here is an adverb, "by what means? in what way? how?" (cf. OLD 1); this usage is rare in classical prose. Note the indirect questions.

prae rubore < *prae*, prep. + abl., usually "in front of, before" but here "in the face of, under the pressure of (an emotion, etc.)," cf. OLD 5a.

inpos < *impos, -otis*, adj. + genitive, "not having control of"; *impos animi* is used regularly to mean "out of one's mind."

13.1. **Raptim:** "hurriedly"; adverb.

paupertina Milonis cenula: *paupertinus, -a, -um,* "poverty-stricken." *cēnula, -ae,* f., "little dinner." Lucius had found Milo's miserly hospitality a problem from the very beginning of his visit, cf. *Met.* 1.23-24.

perfunctus < *perfungor, -ī, -ctus,* "to carry through"; also (esp. in the perfect) "to be finished with something"; construed with the ablative.

causatusque < *causor, -ārī, -ātus,* "plead as an excuse."

concedo: The original meaning of *concedo* is "withdraw, retire," cf. OLD 1a; historical present, cf. AG §469.

cubitum < *cubō, -āre, -uī, -itum,* "to lie down"; supine, cf. AG §509.

abiectus in lectulo meo < *abiciō, -icere, -iēcī, -iectum,* "to throw down, to throw oneself down"; sometimes construed with *in* + ablative, where we would expect *ad* or *in* + accusative (see van der Paardt ad loc.).

13.2. **Fotis**: Fotis is Milo's slave, with whom Lucius has been having an affair. It is probably significant that her name is derived from Greek φῶς ("light"); notice also that Lucius' name may be connected with *lux*.

cubitu < *cubitus, -ūs,* m., "a lying down."

procurato < *prōcūrō, -āre, -āvī, -ātum,* "take care of, attend to."

sui longe dissimilis: "not at all like her normal self"; *dissimilis* can take a genitive (OLD a); cf. AG §349d for the genitive of specification in later authors.

dicaculo < *dicāculus, -a, -um,* "spirited, lively."

vultuosam < *vultuōsus, -a, -um,* "marked by affected or exaggerated facial expression" (OLD); according to van der Paardt the word here has the developed meaning "sad."

adseverabat < *assevērō (adsēverō), -āre, -āvī, -ātum,* here "to make a serious face, put on a stern expression" (OLD 3).

13.4. **licet maius**: "even a bigger one"; literally, "although a bigger one"; *licet* here, as at 3.9.7, has the force of a conjunction.

13.5. **nec tamen me putes**: "But you shouldn't think," "Don't think." The use of the present subjunctive with *nē* to express a prohibition is poetic; classical prose uses only the perfect subjunctive, cf. AG §450. *nec* is used instead of *nē* to join a prohibition to a positive command (cf. OLD *neque* 3b).

concinnasse < *concinnō, -āre, -āvī, -ātum,* "prepare; bring about, cause."

dii mihi melius, quam ut: "Heaven forbid that ..."; literally, "May the gods (grant) something better than that ...." (cf. OLD *melior* 9b). *quam* is used regularly with the the comparative forms of adjectives and adverbs to compare things that are dissimilar (OLD *quam* 8; cf. AG §407). The entire expression is an elaborate version of *utinam* with an optative subjunctive (cf. AG §§441-442).

mei causa: "because of me"; for this use of *causā* + genitive see on 3.11.2.

vel: "even"; cf. OLD 5a.

tantillum < *tantillus, -a, -um,* "so small."

scrupulum < *scrūpulus, -ī,* m., "a source of uneasiness, a worry."

patiare = *patiāris*.

13.6. **quid adversi:** *adversi* is partitive genitive.

respicit: "has reference to" (OLD *respiciō* 9b).

protinus: "at once" (cf. OLD 3), as often in Apuleius.

luatur < *luō, -ere, -ī,* here "atone for, expiate."

sed quod = *sed id quod*.

alterius rei causa: "for a different reason," literally "for the sake of a different thing."

in tuam reccidit iniuriam: "turned out to be harmful to you." < *recidō, -cidere, -c(c)idī, (-cāsum),* "to fall back," but also used for injuries in particular, "to fall out with a particular effect" (OLD 2).

14.1. **familiaris curiositatis admonitus:** The basic meaning of *admoneō* is "to remind someone of something"; it takes a genitive (cf. OLD 1a). Lucius' *curiositas* gets him in trouble throughout the novel, and is a concept central to it.

delitiscentem < *dēlitiscō, -iscere, -uī,* "to hide."

suscipio: "reply"; cf. OLD 2b.

14.2. **tibi verberandae:** The dative of the gerundive is used to express purpose with certain verbs (cf. AG §505); the gerundive in agreement with a noun or pronoun is used regularly in prose instead of the gerund with a direct object (cf. AG §503).

a me: ablative of agent.

plumeam < *plūmeus, -a, -um,* "feathery-soft."

14.3. **quod tuum factum:** *quod* here is the interrogative adjective; it is the direct object of *convertit*.

scaevitas: "bad luck." *scaevitās, -ātis,* f. literally means "instinctive choosing of the wrong, perversity" (OLD); many editors add

Fortunae to the text, but it is easy enough to supply it for ourselves.

consecuta < *consequor, consequī, consecūtus*, "to follow," here almost as an adjective, i.e. "subsequent."

adiuro enim tuum mihi carissimum caput: *adiūrō, -āre, -āvī, -ātum*, here "to swear by" (+ acc.); a Roman would regularly swear by someone's head. The whole expression governs an indirect statement.

quod: introduces a subordinate indirect statement dependent on *credere*; see above on 3.4.4.

14.4. **porro**: "moreover"; adverb (cf. OLD *porrō* 6).

meditatus innoxios: "innocent intentions"; *meditātus, -ūs*, m., is a rare variant of *meditatio*.

culpae non potest addicere: "cannot label as guilt"; literally "cannot assign to (the category of) guilt." *addīcō* is a legal term meaning "to assign something to someone."

14.5. **prona** < *prōnus, -a, -um*, here "eager, willing" (OLD 6b).

marcidos < *marcidus, -a, -um*, "drooping, languid."

adnixis < *adnixus, -a, -um*, "vehement, strenuous" (rare).

sorbillantibus < *sorbillō, -āre, -āvī, -ātum*, "to sip" (rare).

saviis < *sāvium, -iī*, n., "kiss."

15.1. **Patere ... obcludam** = *patere ut obcludam*; *patere* is imperative of *patior*. For the omission of *ut* with a verb of commanding cf. AG, §565a.

petulantia: here "carelessness."

15.2 **pessulis** < *pessulus, -ī*, m., "bolt" (of a door).

uncino < *uncīnus, -ī*, m., "hook."

reversa < *revertor, revertī, reversus*, "return."

inplexa < *implectō (inplectō), implectere, implexī, implexum*, "intertwine" (usually, as here, in the perfect passive participle); here with dative of reference (*colloque meo*) and ablative of means (*manibus ambabus*).

15.4. **sed melius ... praesumo**: "but I have better assumptions about."

natalium < *nātālis, -is*, "natal, native"; in the plural "the circumstances of one's birth," i.e. "parentage" (cf. OLD 7a).

profecto: "undoubtedly"; adverb.

nosti = *novisti*.

15.5. **huius religiosi pectoris tui**: appositional genitive, with *penetralibus* (cf. AG §343d); *tui* is an adjective.

penetralibus < *penetrāle, -is*, "the inner part" (e.g. of a building); "the secret part."

custodias: For the omission of *ut* see on 3.15.1.

simplicitatem: *simplicitās* here means "frankness, candor" (OLD 5).

remunerare < *remūneror, -ārī, -ātus*, "repay."

15.6. **quae sola mortalium novi**: *quae* is probably neuter plural accusative, in agreement with an understood *ea*, the object of *indicare*.

15.7. **erae** < *era, erae*, f., "mistress."

quibus obaudiunt manes: *obaudiō* (rare) means "obey," and takes the dative.

turbantur sidera, coguntur numina, serviunt elementa: These phrases are parallel in construction to *obaudiunt manes*; *quibus* is a dative of reference in each phrase (cf. AG §376-7).

15.8. **magis ... quam**: "more ... than" (cf. OLD *magis* 1b).

nititur < *nītor, nītī, nīxus* or *nīsus*, here "rely on" (+ ablative, cf. OLD 3a).

scitulae < *scītulus, -a, -um*, "good-looking."

formulae < *formula, -ae*, f., "pretty little appearance" (here, rarely, seen as a true diminutive of *forma*); genitive of quality, cf. AG §345.

libenter: "with pleasure, gladly"; adverb.

crebriter: "frequently"; adverb (rare).

16.1. **Boeotium** < *Boeōtius, -a, -um*, "Boeotian." Boeotia is a region of Greece, north of Attica and south of Thessaly. The Boeotians were proverbially rustic and unlettered.

efflictim: "passionately"; adverb (rare).

deperit < *dēpereō, -īre, -iī*, here "die for love of"; "be madly in love with."

totasque artis manus: "all the resources of (her) skill"; *manus* can be used by metonymy to mean "artistic ability," cf. OLD 20b; here the meaning is developed even further, since Pamphyle's skill is that of a magician not an artist.

machinas omnes: parallel to *totas ... manus*; note the asyndeton and chiasmus.

16.2. **vesperi**: *vesperi* means "during the most recent evening," so it usually means "yesterday evening"; since this conversation is taking place at bedtime, *vesperi* here can mean "this evening."

quod ... ruisset ... cessisset: The clause is causal; the subjunctive indicates that the explanation is that offered by someone other than the speaker, cf. AG §540. *cessisset* < *cēdō, cēdere, cessī, cessum*, here "give way to" (of heavenly bodies, cf. OLD 5b).

magiae < *magīa, -ae,* f., "magic" (rare, though common in Apuleius).

comminantem < *comminor, -ārī, -ātus*, "to threaten" someone (dative) with something (accusative).

16.3. **tonstrinae** < *tonstrīna, -ae,* f., "barbershop"; dative with *residentem* (OLD *resideo* 1a).

humi: locative.

diiacebant < *dīiaceō, -ēre, -uī, -itum*, "lie all around"; the word is attested only here, and some scholars read *iacebant*.

clanculo = *clam*, i.e. "secretly"; probably with *ferre* rather than with *praecipitavit*. It was thought that clippings from the body (nails as well as hair) could be used for magical purposes.

16.4. **alioquin**: "otherwise"; "at other times, for other reasons"; adverb.

publicitus: "publicly"; adverb.

perinfames < *perinfāmis, -e*, "very notorious" (rare).

16.5. **ultima** < *ultimus, -a, -um*, here "lowest, meanest" (OLD 9b).

subinde: here "repeatedly"; adverb.

lectorum iuvenum: "of respectable young men"; < *lectus, -a, -um*, here "excellent, choice," a word regularly applied to *iuvenis*.

constanter: "firmly, without ado"; adverb, as at 3.3.9.

obiciam < *obiciō, ob(i)icere, obiēcī, obiectum*, here "hand over (for prosecution)," OLD 5.

16.6 **scrutatus** < *scrūtor, -ārī, -ātus*, "search, search for."

16.7. **gesto** < *gestum, -ī*, n., "deed, business."

repulsa: "defeat" (ablative).

tui contemplatione: *tui* is objective genitive, cf. AG §348.

17.1. **ne ... rediem**: a clause of fearing, dependent on the implications of *tristis*.

conspicor: *conspicor* is historical present, which takes either primary or (as here) secondary sequence; cf. AG §485e.

forficulis < *forficulae, -ārum,* f. pl., "scissors."

caprinos < *caprīnus, -a, -um,* "of goats."

17.2. **quos cum ... cernerem** = *cum eos ... cernerem*; for the use of a relative pronoun at the beginning of a clause to connect it with a preceding one cf. AG §308f.

probe: "correctly"; adverb. Someone had done a good job of pulling together and inflating the wineskins.

capillos eorum: *capillī* are usually the hairs of a human's head, but Fotis is of course thinking of the use to which she will put the wool cut from the wineskins.

flavos < *flāvus, -a, -um,* "yellow, blond."

per hoc: "for this reason," i.e. because the goat hairs were *flavi*, though Fotis did not actually say that the young man was blond. For *per* "as a result of" cf. OLD 13a.

illi Boeotio iuveni consimiles = *illius Boeotii iuvenis capillis consimiles.*

plusculos < *plusculus, -a, -um,* "a fairly large number of."

17.3. **priusquam cena te reciperes** < *recipiō, -ere, -cēpī, -ceptum,* "to bring oneself back," i.e. "to return." It can take both reflexive as direct object, and a simple ablative to express the place from which someone returns, cf. OLD 12a.

vecors: *vēcors, vēcordis,* "mad, deranged."

animi: *animus* is regularly used with words of feeling in what looks like the genitive case (really locative); cf. AG §358.

scandulare < *scandulāris, -e,* "made of shingles."

quod: The antecedent is *tectum.*

altrinsecus: "on the other side"; adverb, here + genitive.

patore < *pator, -ōris,* m., "an opening."

perflabili < *perflābilis, -is, -e,* "open to the wind"; literally, "able to be blown through."

orientales ceterosque: The eastern direction is singled out because the East was particularly important in magic.

colit < *colō, colere, coluī, cultum,* "inhabit," or perhaps here "maintain," cf. OLD 4a.

17.4. **priusque ... instruit:** We might have expected the pluperfect, since these preparations presumably took place before the visit in question, but the perfect perhaps reflects the excited narrative style of Fotis ("she went up ... she has previously equipped ...").

omne genus aromatis: "with spices of every kind." *arōma, -atis,* n., "spice" is third declension, but has as its ablative plural *arōmatīs*;

omne genus is an adverbial phrase, an idiomatic usage of the word *genus*, cf. OLD 13 (also AG §397a).

ignorabiliter: "unintelligibly"; adverb.

lamminis litteratis < *lāmina (lammina)*, -ae, f., "a thin sheet of metal, a plate." These "inscribed plates" are curse tablets (*tabellae defixionum*). A number of these survive from the ancient world; their use is described in Tacitus' account of the death of Germanicus (*Ann.* 2.69).

infelicium navium durantibus damnis < *dūrō*, -āre, -āvī, -ātum, here "survive" (cf. OLD 7c); < *damnum*, -ī, n., "a loss," here "a lost possession, a part" (OLD 3b). Materials from shipwrecks (especially ropes) were used in magic. Scholars have also proposed reading *infelicium avium*.

17.5. **defletorum** < *dēfleō*, -ēre, -ēvī, -ētum, "to mourn"; thus a *defletus* (substantivized participle) is a corpse. The use of human remains for magical purposes is also attested in Tacitus, *Ann.* 2.69.

admodum: "to a great extent"; (modifying an adjective) "very, quite, rather"; adverb.

carnosi clavi: "spikes with flesh on them"; < *clāvus*, -ī, m., "a nail; a spike."

pendentium: "of executed criminals"; < *pendeō*, -ēre, pependī, "to be suspended, to hang"; the word is used on its own for those suffering traditional Roman punishments, such as crucifixion, cf. OLD 2a.

trucidatorum < *trucīdō*, -āre, -āvī, -ātum, "to slaughter."

servatus cruor: "preserved gore"; for the use of *servō, servāre* to describe the preservation of perishables cf. OLD 7b.

dentibus ferarum: *dentibus* is ablative of separation, cf. AG §402.

trunca < *truncus*, -a, -um, "mutilated."

calvaria < *calvāria*, -ium, n. pl., "skulls."

18.1. **decantatis spirantibus fibris:** ablative absolute, with *spirantibus* treated as an adjective. < *fibra*, -ae, f., "a leaf," but in the plural "entrails."

litat < *litō*, -āre, -āvī, -ātum, here in its basic meaning of "make (acceptable) sacrifice" (intransitive).

vario latice < *latex*, -icis, m., originally "water," but here "liquid" (in general); ablative of instrument with *litat*.

rore fontano: "spring water"; < *rōs, roris*, m., originally "dew," but here "water," cf. OLD 2a.

vaccino < *vaccīnus, -a, -um,* "of the cow."

libat < *lībō, -āre, -āvī, -ātum,* "to pour a libation."

mulsa < *mulsum, -ī,* n., "mead" (i.e. a drink made from honey and wine).

18.2. **mutuos nexus:** "reciprocal knots" (here of hair).

obditos < *obdō, -dere, -didī, -ditum,* "to block, to shut; to restrain," i.e. "to tie up." Witches made knots for magical purposes, cf. Virgil, *Eclogue* 8.78-79.

carbonibus < *carbō, -ōnis,* m., "a (piece of) charcoal."

adolendos < *adoleō, adolēre, adultum,* "make a burnt offering"; "burn."

18.3 **illa corpora:** What Fotis calls "bodies" are of course really the wineskins.

18.4. **exuviarum** < *exuviae, -ārum,* f. pl., "spoils"; often the armor taken from a dead enemy, but also the hair, skin, fingernails, etc. used in magic.

pro illo iuvene Boeotio: *pro* here means "instead of, as a substitute for" (cf. OLD 6a).

aditum gestientes: "eagerly desiring entrance"; *gestiō* in this sense usually takes an infinitive rather than, as here, a simple accusative.

18.5. **cum:** introduces another *cum inversum* construction, for which see on 3.9.1 above.

crapula < *crāpula, -ae,* f., "drunkenness."

improvidae < *improvīdus, -a, -um,* "unseeing"; transferred epithet.

in insani modum Aiacis: Ajax went mad with resentment when Odysseus was awarded the arms of the dead Achilles; in one night he slaughtered the flocks of the Greeks, and then killed himself.

18.6. **laniavit** < *laniō, -āre, -āvī, -ātum,* "tear up."

sed longe fortius: If the text is sound, there is an anacolouthon (breakdown of syntax); we need to supply here something like *armenta laniavisti.*

18.7. **utricidam** < *utricīda, -ae,* m. The word is made up by Apuleius, from *uter, utris,* m., "(leather) bag; wineskin." The joke works perfectly well in English: "not a homicide, but a bagicide."

19.1. **Risi lepido sermone:** *rīdeō* can be construed with an ablative of cause, cf. OLD 5a.

cavillatus < *cavillor, -ārī, -ātus,* "to jest, to banter."

Ergo igitur: The pleonasm is frequent in Apuleius.

mihi: dative of reference, cf. AG §378.

adoriam < *adōria, -ae,* f., "glory, distinction."

ad exemplum ... numerare: "class as a parallel"; cf. OLD *numerō* 8.

duodeni laboris Herculei: *duodēnī, -ae, -a* means "distributed into twelve parts"; the more normal expression would be *duodecim laborum*.

19.2. **trigemino corpori Geryonis**: Stealing the cattle of Geryon was one of the twelve labors of Hercules; Geryon had three heads and three bodies as far as his waist.

triplici formae Cerberi: The eleventh labor of Hercules was to bring back Cerberus from the underworld; Cerberus, the dog who guarded the entrance to Hades, had three heads. The emphasis on the three-fold nature of Geryon and Cerberus is of course due to the fact that Lucius had supposedly killed *three* robbers.

coaequando: The gerund in the ablative can be used to express manner; in late writers such as Apuleius the construction is virtually the equivalent of a present participle; cf. AG §507. This usage survives in Italian: *sto dicendo* means "I am in the process of saying."

19.3. **ex animo**: "heartily" (cf. OLD *animus* 8b).

volens: modifies the subject of *remittam*.

praesta quod = *praesta illud quod*; on the omission of the antecedent of a relative pronoun cf. AG §307c.

19.4. **videam**: As the text stands, this must be either a hortatory subjunctive (AG §439) or an optative subjunctive (AG §441), used to express a wish; it may be that the text should read <ut> *videam*.

coram: here the adverb, "face to face, before my very eyes."

19.5. **expers** < *expers, expertis,* adj., "lacking knowledge."

scio istud: i.e. "I know that you know a lot about magic."

cum: introduces a long causal clause: *cum ... teneas <me> volentem*.

spretorem < *sprētor, sprētōris,* m., "one who despises" (rare).

matronalium < *mātrōnālis, -e,* "of a married woman," but here perhaps "of women" (in general). The word may also suggest that the women in question are respectable women rather than slaves like Fotis.

amplexuum < *amplexus, -ūs,* m., "embrace."

bucculis < *buccula, -ae,* f., "cheek."

osculis < *osculum, -ī,* n., here "lips" (OLD 2a).

fraglantibus = *flagrantibus,* "burning."

Apuleius, *Metamorphoses* III

addictum < *addīcō, -īcere, -ixī, -ictum*, "assign custody," hence "to enslave" (cf. OLD 6b).

mancipatum < *mancipō, -āre, āvī, -ātum*, "to transfer, to sell" (esp. as a slave). Both *addictum* and *mancipatum* mean "enslaved"; the former is more general, the term refers to an explicit judicial process.

19.6. **larem** < *Lar, -ris*, m., "household god" and therefore "home." Lucius is only a visitor in Hypata, and might well, given his recent experiences, have thought about going home to Corinth.

domuitionem < *domuitio, -ōnis*, f., "a homeward journey."

nocte ista nihil antepono: *antepono* here means "prefer" (one thing to another), construed with an accusative (for the thing preferred) and an ablative (for the thing not preferred).

20.1. **quam vellem:** Exclamatory *quam* can modify verbs, as at 3.12.3.

praeter invidos mores: i.e. aside from the fact that she is generally disagreeable; *invidus, -a, -um* can mean "malevolent, hostile."

in solitudinem: "in order to obtain solitude" (cf. OLD *in* 21).

abstrusa < *abstrūsus, -a, -um*, "hidden."

viduata < *viduō, -āre, -āvī, -ātum*, "deprive (of)" + ablative.

20.2. **modo:** "only"; adverb (very common).

ut initio praefata sum: Fotis said this at 3.15.5.

20.3. **garrientibus** < *garriō, -īre*, "to chatter."

20.4. **amiculis** < *amīculum, -ī*, n., "wrap, mantle."

hactenus: normally means "so far" or "to this extent," but in Apuleius it can mean "completely" or "all the way" (adverb).

bacchamur < *bacchor, -ārī, -ātum*, "to celebrate the rites of Bacchus," hence "to act like a Bacchante, to rave, to rage" (OLD 3a).

in Venerem: "for Venus" (cf. OLD *in* 11a).

puerile obtulit corollarium: "she offered the boy's bonus." *puerīlis, -e* can mean "pertaining to sodomy," cf. OLD 2 and Martial 9.67.3: *fessus mille modis illud puerile poposci. corollārium, -(i)ī*, n., means "a garland," but also "an extra payment, a bonus."

vigilia: ablative; here "wakefulness."

etiam in altum diem: *in* here means "until", cf. OLD 13b; *altus, -a, -um* here means "late," a usage occuring only in Apuleius (OLD 8b).

attinuit: The basic meaning of *attineō* is "to hold" or "keep hold of."

21.1. **ad hunc modum**: For this meaning of *ad* + accusative ("in" a way) cf. OLD 36a.

voluptarie: "for pleasure, pleasurably"; adverb.

percita < *percieō, -iēre, -iī, -itum*, "to set in motion; to excite (feelings, etc.)."

nihil ... promoveret: "she was making no headway" (OLD *prōmoveō* 5a).

in avem: "so as to become a bird"; for this use of *in* + acc. cf. OLD 19a.

sese plumaturam: sc. *esse*.

21.2. **proin**: (pronounced as one syllable) "so then, accordingly"; adverb.

memet: a strengthened form of *mē*.

speculam < *specula, -ae*, f., here "the act of spying, observation."

21.3. **circa primam noctis vigiliam**: "around the first watch of the night"; *vigilia* here means "a watch," i.e. one of four divisions of the night to which night watchmen were assigned (OLD 2).

suspenso: *suspendō* with words like *pedem* and *vestigium* can mean "to go on tiptoe."

insono < *insonus, -a, -um*, "soundless" (rare).

vestigio: *vestigium* means not only "footprint, track" but also "step."

rimam < *rīma, -ae*, f., "crack."

ostiorum < *ostium, -(i)ī*, n., "door."

arbitrari: *arbitror* here in its original meaning of "observe" (cf. OLD 1).

sic: "as follows" (cf. OLD 3a).

21.4. **laciniis** < *lacinia, -ae*, f., normally "fringe, hem," but also, in the plural, "clothes" (OLD 2b).

arcula < *arcula, -ae*, f., "a small chest, a box."

reclusa < *reclūdō, reclūdere, reclūdī, reclūsum*, "to open."

pyxides < *pyxis, pyxidis*, f., "small box, casket" (esp. for medicines, cosmetics, etc.).

de quis: *quīs* is a common alternative form of *quibus*.

operculo < *operculum, -ī*, n., "a cover, a cap."

indidem: "from the same place"; adverb.

Apuleius, *Metamorphoses* III

egesta < *ēgerō, -erere, -essī, -estum*, "to take out; to extract" (OLD 2a).

unguedine < *unguēdō, -inis*, f., "an ointment, unguent."

adfricta < *affricō (adfricō), adfricāre, adfricuī, adfrictum*, "rub on."

adusque: "all the way to, right up to"; adverb and preposition.

cum lucerna secreto conlocuta: *colloquor (conloquor)* means "to have a discussion with someone" and takes *cum* + abl; *secreto* is an adverb, meaning "separately," "privately," or "softly." Lamps were regularly used in magic, and Pamphyle is depicted as treating her lamp as a kind of collaborator.

succussu < *succussus, -ūs*, m., "a shaking, a jolting."

21.5. **quis leniter fluctuantibus**: *quīs* = *quibus*; the antecedent is *membra* in the previous sentence.

promicant: *promico* means "to start out, shoot forward," as at 3.10.3.

nasus incurvus: *incurvus, -a, -um* "crooked, bent"; here presumably "having become bent."

coguntur: *cogo* here means "to compress, to form something by compression" (cf. OLD 8a).

adunci < *aduncus, -a, -um*, "hooked, curved."

21.6. **bubo** < *būbō, -ōnis*, m./f., "a horned owl"; it has a disturbing cry, and was considered a bird of ill-omen, and one into which a witch might transform herself.

sic: "thus" in the sense of "in this case"; instead of pointing to a specific action (the basic meaning of *sic*), it sums up the situation in general.

periclitabunda < *perīclitābundus, -a, -um*, "testing"; here with the genitive.

resultat < *resultō, -āre*, "to jump away from a position" (OLD 1).

sublimata < *sublīmō, -āre, -āvī, -ātum*, "rise, soar."

forinsecus: "outside, out"; adverb.

totis alis: "in full flight"; *totus, -a, -um* when applied to parts of the body in the ablative of instrument can mean "making full use of" them, cf. OLD 3d.

22.1. **reformatur** < *reformō, -āre, -āvī, -ātum*, "to change" (without any implication of repetition).

praesentis ... facti: objective genitive, cf. AG §348.

22.2. **sic exterminatus animi**: "so astonished ... that." < *exterminō*,

-*āre, -āvī, -ātum*, "to banish," thus "driven out of my mind"; *sīc* in this sense is normally followed by a result clause with *ut* + subjunctive, but Apuleius often prefers parallel constructions to subordinate ones.

attonitus in amentiam: "frightened out of my wits"; for *in* + acc. "so as to produce" (a given condition) cf. OLD 20.

adeo diu: "so long ... (that)"; *adeō*, when used in this sense, normally takes a result clause with *ut* + subjunctive, but Apuleius' preference for parataxis is again at work.

pupulis < *pūpula, -ae*, f., "a little girl," hence "the pupil of the eye" (because if you are a woman and look into someone's eye, you see a little woman reflected back at you).

an vigilarem = *num vigilarem*; in later Latin *an* is regularly used instead of *num*.

22.3. **sensum praesentium:** "awareness of present realities"; *praesentium* is neuter plural genitive of praesens.

meis luminibus: Lucius moves Fotis' hand to his eyes in order to invoke them as witnesses and pledges for his request; see on 3.7.2 above.

22.4. **Patere:** from *patior*, as at 3.15.1.

magno et singulari ... adfectionis tuae fructu: Note that *magno* and *singulari* modify *fructu*; this radical displacement of words is a rhetorical figure known as hyperbaton.

22.5. **impertire** < *impertior, -īrī*, "to impart; to communicate; to bestow," a deponent form of the more common *impertio*.

nobis: Latin regularly uses what we call the royal we "to convey a formal, impersonal, or self-deprecatory tone" (OLD *nōs* 3a).

unctulum < *unctulum, -ī*, n., "a dab of ointment."

per istas tuas papillas: *per* + accusative is regularly used in oaths and earnest requests, cf. OLD 10. Scholars have been tempted to emend to *pupillas*, since, as we have seen, it was normal to invoke eyes in oaths and entreaties, but Apuleius is offering a racier alternative.

mellitula: vocative of *mellitula, -ae*, f., "honey."

mancipium: originally "formal ownership," but also "slave."

tibi perpetuo pignera: "bind to yourself forever." *pignerō, -āre, -āvī, -ātum*: "to pledge; to bind" (by an obligation); OLD 2a.

Cupido pinnatus adsistam: *Cupido* is in apposition with "I," the subject of *adsistam*. Lucius' comparison is odd, or funny: he concentrates on the fact that Cupid has wings, and ignores the fact that Cupid's relationship with his mother was very different from the sexual one imagined here.

22.6. **Ain** = *aisne*, i.e. "you don't say!" (OLD *āiō* 2).

vulpinaris < *vulpīnor, -ārī*, "to be foxy, crafty."

amasio < *amāsiō, -ōnis*, m., "a lover," but more dismissive; translate, perhaps, "lover boy."

sponte asceam cruribus meis inlidere: "to strike an axe against my legs," i.e. "to shoot myself in the foot." < *ascia, -ae* or *ascea, -ae*, f., "an axe"; < *illīdō (inlīdō), -dere, sī, -sum*, "to crush; to beat, to strike."

sic: "as things are now" (cf. OLD 1b); i.e. without any magical transformations on Lucius' part.

inermem < *inermis, -e*, "unarmed"; modifies an understood *te*.

a lupulis ... Thessalis: "from those Thessalian whores." < *lupula, -ae*, f., "a prostitute." The word is used here as a general term of abuse for the local women; one gathers that Fotis is not a native of the region.

alitem factum: "made into a bird."

quaeram: Sc. *tē* as direct object.

23.1. **At ... depellant**: *at* is used to introduce exclamations or entreaties, cf. OLD 11; *depellant* is optative subjunctive, cf. AG §441.

ut ego ... non ... devolem: The *ut* clause is in apposition with *scelus istud*.

volatibus < *volātus, -ūs*, m., "a flight."

pervius: normally "passable, accessible" but here with a rare active sense, i.e. "making one's way through" (OLD 4).

supremi Iovis certus nuntius: Jupiter often used an eagle as his messenger.

armiger: *armiger, -erī*, m., "armor-bearer, squire"; here Jupiter's eagle, who carried his thunderbolts.

nidulum < *nīdulus, -ī*, m., "little nest."

subinde: *subinde* can mean both "thereupon" and "repeatedly"; either meaning is possible here, though the former seems preferable, picking up *post illam pinnarum dignitatem*.

23.2. **nodulum** < *nōdulus, -ī*, m., "little knot." For the invocation of a person's *caput* in oaths see above on 3.14.3 *adiuro ... tuum caput*; there may also be an allusion to the importance of knots in magic; see on 3.18.2.

vinxisti < *vinciō, vincīre, vinxī, victum*, "to tie up, bind."

23.3. **tunc etiam** = *praeterea*.

avem talem ... induero = *formam avis talis induero*. < *induō, induere, induī, indūtum*, "to put on (a garment, etc.)."

domus omnis: accusative plural; direct object of *vitare*.

me: *me* is the subject of *debere*, the infinitive of an indirect statement depending on *istud meis cogitationibus occurrit*.

quam pulchro enim: In classical Latin the normal position for *enim* is second in a sentence, but Apuleius often has it third.

perfruentur < *perfruor, perfruī, perfructus*, "enjoy" (+ ablative).

23.4. **quid, quod**: "what of the fact that?" cf. OLD s.v. *quod* 4e.

sollicite: "anxiously"; adverb.

foribus videmus adfigi: The custom of nailing birds to doorposts as apotropaic devices is referred to by Roman authors, and survived in Italy and elsewhere into the 20th century.

quod ... familiae minantur: The antecedent of *quod* is *exitium*, i.e. the (destruction) with which they threaten the household." < *minor, -ārī, -ātus*, "to threaten," with both a direct object (the punishment that one threatens) and an indirect object (the person one threatens with punishment). The point is that some birds, because they were ill-omened, were threatening by their very presence (*infaustis volatibus*).

cruciatibus < *cruciātus, -ūs*, m., "torture" or "agony." The birds will pay with their own sufferings for the fact that they threatened the household; the nailing up of birds is seen as a kind of crucifixion, the normal Roman method of execution for criminals of low status.

23.5. **sciscitari** < *sciscitor, -ārī, -ātus*, "inquire, try to find out about."

23.6. **Bono animo es**: *es* is imperative.

quod ad huius rei curam pertinet: For this use of *quod* to introduce a new clause, not grammatically related to the main sentence, cf. OLD 6a; translate "for what pertains ..."

singula: neuter plural accusative.

23.7. **nec istud factum putes**: Sc. *esse*; for the tense of the subjunctive see above on 3.13.5.

medela < *medēla, -ae*, f., "a medicine, a cure."

possem: For the use of an imperfect subjunctive in a subordinate clause in indirect discourse when the main verb is in the present tense, an apparent violation of the sequence of tenses, cf. AG §585a.

Apuleius, *Metamorphoses* III

subsistere < *subsistō, -sistere, -stitī*, here "to assist, to come with relief to a person" (+ dative and ablative of means), cf. OLD 2.

23.8. **futtilibus** < *futtilis, -is, -e*, "insignificant."

anethi < *anēthum, -ī*, n., "dill."

rori < *rōs, rōris*, m., here "water," as at 3.18.1.

fontano < *fontānus, -a, -um*, "from a spring."

datur: For the use of *dō* to mean "administer" (of medicines etc.) cf. OLD 9b.

lavacrum et poculum: predicate nominatives, cf. AG §284. *lavācrum, -ī*, n., "bath" (rare); *pōculum, -ī*, n., "a drink."

24.2. **quam:** The antecedent is *pyxidem* in the previous sentence; for the use of a relative pronoun at the beginning of a sentence to connect it with what precedes cf. AG §308f.

amplexus < *amplector, amplectī, amplexus*, "to embrace."

deosculatus < *deosculor, -ārī, -ātus*, "to kiss warmly."

utque ... deprecatus: *deprecor* ("to pray") regularly takes *ut* + subjunctive; *faveo* ("to be favorable to") takes a dative.

propere: "quickly"; adverb.

haurito < *hauriō, -rīre, -sī (-riī), -stum (-rītum)*, "to draw" (of liquids like water), but also "to scoop up," used even of solids (cf. OLD 4a).

plusculo < *plusculus, -a, -um*, "quite a lot of."

uncto < *unctum, -ī*, n., "ointment."

perfricui < *perfricō, -āre, -āvī, -ātum*, "rub all over."

24.3. **conatibus** < *cōnātus, -ūs*, m., "attempt."

in avem similem gestiebam: "I was agitating myself into a something like a bird." < *gestiō, -īre, -īvī* or *-iī*: "to long for; to itch with impatience; to exult; to make gestures"; the last meaning seems the one required here, recalling the word's etymology, i.e. *gestus facere*. For the use of *similis* in comparisons, often with almost adverbial force, cf. OLD 2.

plumulae < *plūmula, -ae*, f., "little feather."

pinnulae < *pinnula, -ae*, f., "little wing, feather."

24.4. **pili** < *pilus, -ī*, m., "a hair."

crassantur < *crassō, -āre, -āvī, -ātum*, "to thicken" (rare).

in setas < *saeta, -ae*, f., (also *sēta, -ae*), "bristle"; for the use of *in* + acc. to indicate the substance into which something changes, cf. OLD 19a.

cutis < *cutis, cutis,* f., "skin."

corium < *corium, -(i)ī,* n., "the hide (of an animal)."

24.5. **prolixum** < *prōlixus, -a, -um,* "extensive; tall; long."

horripilant < *horripilō, -āre,* "to become hairy."

auctibus < *auctus, -ūs,* m., "an increase."

24.6. **iam nequeunti tenere Fotidem**: *teneō* can mean "hold in an embrace" (OLD 2b); as a jackass Lucius was now unable to embrace Fotis.

natura: *nātūra, -ae,* f., can mean "natural endowments," i.e. "private parts" (OLD 15). The jackass was notorious in antiquity not just for stubborness and stupidity, but also, because its member is prominent, for male lust.

25.1. **salutis inopia**: literally "with a complete absence of resource," i.e. "helplessly"; *inopia* here is perhaps ablative of description, cf. AG §415.

privatus < *prīvō, -āre, -āvī, -ātum,* "deprive of" (+ ablative).

quod solum poteram: *quod* introduces a clause which amplifies the main sentence; cf. OLD *quod* 2c.

postrema deiecta labia: *postrēmus, -a, -um* can mean "the last part of, the end of" (OLD 3c); putting out the lower lip is of course a typical gesture of unhappiness, but note that donkeys also have prominent lower lips.

oblicum < *oblīquus, -a, -um (oblīcus, -a, -um)*, "oblique"; (of glances) "sidelong"; here a substantivized neuter, i.e. a sidelong glance, indicating slyness or trickery of some kind (OLD 4).

25.3. **sed bene**: i.e. *sed bene est,* "it is well," cf. OLD *bene* 8b.

facilior: For the use of the comparative as a kind of ironic positive see on 3.10.5 above.

reformationis < *reformātiō, -ōnis,* f., "transformation, metamorphosis."

suppeditat < *suppeditō, -āre, -āvī, -ātum,* here "to be available" (as a resource), OLD 1c.

demorsicatis < *dēmorsicō, -āre, -āvī, -ātum,* "to nibble at."

exibis asinum: "you will depart from (the shape of) the donkey"; *exeō* can mean "go beyond, exceed the limits of" (OLD 13a).

postliminio: "by the right of return"; *postliminium* is a technical term for the restoration of legal rights to a Roman citizen upon return from capture by foreigners.

25.4. atque utinam ... parassem: *atque* is used here not as a connective but to introduce an emphatic sentence, cf. OLD 2a; *utinam* is often used to introduce an optative subjunctive, cf. AG §442.

vesperi: "this (past) evening"; see above on 3.16.2.

de more: "in the usual way"; a common idiom, cf. OLD *mōs* 3a.

moram talem: "such a difficult delay"; for the use of *talis* to mean "of such an exceptional character" (bad as well as good) cf. OLD 3a.

patereris: imperfect subjunctive of *patior* in the apodosis of a contrary to fact condition, in which the the protasis has been replaced by the optative subjunctive, cf. AG §521b.

noctis unius: perhaps best defined as an appositional genitive, cf. AG §343d.

diluculo < *dīlūculum, -ī*, n., "dawn."

26.1. perfectus asinus: a pun, since Lucius is now a "complete jackass" in both the literal and the figurative sense.

iumentum < *iūmentum, -ī*, n., "beast of burden."

26.2. spissis < *spissus, -a, -um*, "dense," thus "thick and fast" (OLD 4).

calcibus < *calx, calcis*, f., "the heel," thus "a kick."

26.3. temerario < *temerārius, -a, -um*, "rash; reckless."

suppetias < *suppetiae, -ārum*, f. pl., "assistance."

rursus: here "on top of that, in addition" (cf. OLD 5a); adverb.

26.4. demussata temporali contumelia: i.e. "swallowing the temporary insult" (ablative absolute). < *dēmussō, -āre, -āvī, -ātum*, "to mutter, to swallow in silence"; *temporalis* can mean "temporary" (OLD 2a).

casui < *casus, casūs*, m., here, as often, "misfortune, disaster" (cf OLD 5).

serviens < *serviō, -īre, -īvi* or *iī, -ītum*, "to serve (as a slave); to submit oneself to something" (+ dat.).

vectorem < *vector, -ōris*, m., "beast"; literally, "one who transports."

26.5. rebar < *reor, rērī, ratus*, "to think."

si quod inesset: "if there was any ... in"; *quod* is here an indefinite adjective, as often with *sī* (cf. OLD *quī, quae, quod* 25a). For the rules of contrary to fact conditions in indirect discourse cf. AG §589b.

sacramentum: "obligation," as at 3.3.8.

agnitione < *agnitiō, -ōnis*, f., "recognition."

loca lautia: "an official welcome"; *loca lautia praebere* is a technical term for the act of providing official entertainment to foreign ambassadors at Rome.

praebiturum: sc. *fuisse*; for the apodosis of contrary to fact conditions in indirect discourse cf. AG §589.

26.6. **pro Iuppiter hospitalis:** "by Juppiter the god of hospitality!"; *prō* is an interjection governing the vocative. Juppiter, like Zeus, was the protector of the sacred obligations of guest-friendship.

Fidei secreta numina: "by remote spirits of Loyalty!"; *secretus, -a, -um* has its original meaning here of "remote." The point is that the spirits (*numina*) of Fides are remote from men in these immoral modern times.

praeclarus ... conferunt: Correct grammar would require *confert* instead of *conferunt*, but *cum asino* suggests an additional subject of the sentence; for this violation of the strict rules of noun/verb agreement (rare in classical prose) cf. AG §280a and the notes to §286a and §317.

in meamque perniciem: For *in* + acc. to express purpose, cf. OLD 21a.

26.7. **verentes scilicet cibariis suis** < *cibāria, -ōrum*, n. pl., "rations"; *vereor* can take a dative of the thing for which fear is felt, cf. OLD 3b. *scilicet* ("no doubt") is used to emphasize the fact that the speaker is making assumptions about motives.

vix me praesepio videre proximantem: "scarcely did they see me approaching the manger"; < *praesēpium, -(i)ī*, n., "a cattle stall, manger"; *vidēre* = *vidērunt*; < *proximō, -āre, -āvī, -ātum*, "to approach" (rare; here with the dative).

insecuntur = *insequuntur*.

26.8. **abigor** < *abigō, -ere, -ēgī, -actum*, "drive away."

quam procul: "as far away as possible"; *quam* can give a superlative force to certain adverbs (OLD 3b).

ab ordeo < *hordeum (ordeum), -ī*, n., "barley."

gratissimo: Lucius is here sarcastic.

27.1. **adfectus** < *afficiō, afficere, affēcī, affectum*, here "to harm" (cf. OLD 5).

angulo stabuli concesseram: As at 3.13.1, *concedo* has its original sense of "withdraw"; construed here (probably) with a dative.

27.2. **pilae ... meditullio:** "in practically the very center of the middle pillar, which was holding up the roof-beams of the stable." < *pila*,

-ae, f., "a (squared) pillar"; genitive, dependent on *in ipso fere meditullio*. < *trabs, trabis*, f., here "beam." < *meditullium, -(i)ī*, n., "the interior; the center of a thing" (rare).

Eponae deae: Epona, originally a Celtic goddess, was associated by the Romans with horses and mules. She is not often mentioned in Latin literature, but some forty monuments survive, mostly from N. Italy, Gaul, and the Rhine and Danube provinces.

aediculae < *aedicula, -ae*, f., "a small shrine"; here dative with *residentem*.

accurate: "carefully"; adverb.

equidem recentibus: "and even fresh ones"; now that he is a donkey, Lucius has a gastronomic interest in flowers. In classical Latin the adverb *equidem* is used to emphasize a first person singular subject, but here it simply emphasizes *recentibus* (OLD 2).

27.3. **pronus spei**: "inclined towards hope"; for *pronus* + genitive (rare) cf. OLD 6a.

nimiumque porrectis labiis: *nimium* here means "very much" (cf. OLD 2).

nisu < *nīsus, nīsūs*, m., here "effort."

27.4. **quod**: the direct object of *me ... conantem*; connecting relative.

pessima scilicet sorte: "with remarkably bad luck"; < *sors, sortis*, f., "lot, chance," here referring to the way things turn out (cf. OLD 8a).

27.5. **Quo usque tandem**: the first words of Cicero's first Catilinarian oration, so basic a text in Roman education that quoting is probably merely pretentious.

cantherium < *cantherius, -(i)ī*, m., "a gelding"; also used more generally of a horse (and thus donkey) not worth very much. Lucius, as a donkey, is actually threatened with gelding later in the story (*Met*. 7.23-24).

27.6. **quin**: The basic meaning of *quīn* is "why not?" in direct questions; it is also used to introduce any statement that corroborates or amplifies a previous one, i.e. "in fact" (cf. OLD A2).

sacrilegum < *sacrilegus, -a, -um*, "guilty of sacrilege"; note that the original meaning of *sacrilegium* was not sacrilege in general, but robbery of temples in particular.

temere: "thoughtlessly, by chance"; adverb. Construe with *positum*.

fascem < *fascis, -is*, m., "bundle."

offendit < *offendō, -ere, -dī, -sum*, "to strike against; bump into; come upon, find."

27.7. **rimatusque** < *rīmor, -ārī, -ātus*, "to examine, rummage about for" (OLD 1c).

fustem < *fustis, -is*, m., "stick, club."

largo < *largus, -a, um*, here "plentiful, copious."

viciniae < *vicinia, -ae*, f., "neighborhood."

conclamatis latronibus: "with robbers having been shouted about"; perhaps better printed *conclamatis "latronibus,"* i.e. "with the shout of 'robbers!' having been made."

28.1. **Nec mora**: "all at once," as at 3.2.1.

globus: "a compact round mass; a sphere," but also a technical term for a band of soldiers (cf. OLD 4a).

domus membra < *membrum, -ī*, n., "organ, limb," but also "part" of a house (cf. OLD 3ab); *domūs* is genitive.

convolantibus < *convolō, -āre, -āvī, -ātum*, "to assemble rapidly, to flock together."

discursus hostilis: literally "a hostile dispersal," i.e. "running enemies"; periphrasis for "the robbers."

28.2. **in modum**: "in the manner of" (cf. OLD *modus* 11c).

ortivi < *ortīvus, -a, -um*, "rising."

ignis et mucro: the subjects of *coruscat*; two singular subjects normally take a plural verb unless they are connected by disjunctives (*neque ... neque*), but they are sometimes, as here, treated as a single concept ("fire and sword"), cf. AG §317b.

28.3. **horreum** < *horreum, -ī*, n., normally "storehouse, granary" but here "treasure-room."

obseptum < *obsaepiō (obsēpiō), -īre, -sī, -tum*, "to block, to obstruct."

obseratumque < *obserō, -āre, -āvī, -ātum*, "to place a bar across (a door), to bar."

gazis < *gaza, -ae*, f., "treasure." The word is apparently Persian, and is used in particular of exotic Eastern treasures.

refertum < *refertus, -a, -um*, "crammed, crowded."

securibus < *secūris, secūris*, f., "ax."

diffindunt < *diffindō, -ndere, -dī, -ssum*, "to divide, split."

28.4. **recluso** < *reclūdō, -dere, -sī, -sum*, "to open; open up."

sarcinis < *sarcina, -ae*, f., "bundle"; ablative of means.

28.5. gestaminum modus: "the quantity of the loads." *gestāmen, -inis*, n., "something worn; a load" ; *modus* here means "size, number" (cf. OLD 3a).

gerulorum < *gerulus, -ī*, m., "a porter" .

opulentiae nimiae nimio < *nimius, -a, -um*, "excessive"; < *nimium, -(i)ī*, n., "an excessive amount." The language here is itself clearly excessive.

incitas < *incitae, -ārum*, f. pl., "a checkmate, a stymie" (in a board game).

28.6. domo iam vacua: Remember that *domus, -ī* is feminine.

baculis < *baculum, -ī*, n., "a staff, a stick."

exigunt: *exigō* here has its original sense of "drive out" (OLD 1a).

unoque ... relicto: ablative absolute.

inquisitione < *inquīsītiō, -ōnis*, f., "search; official inquiry." i.e. he would report on the investigation which would follow the assault on Milo's house.

nos: accusative; object of *tundentes* and *ducunt*.

crebra < *crēber, -bra, -brum*, "frequent; numerous; crowded"; the neuter plural is here adverbial.

per avia < *āvius, -a; -um*, "lacking roads, trackless"; here a substantivized neuter.

concitos < *concitus, -a, -um*, "moving rapidly, headlong"; or possibly < *conciēō, -iēre, -īvī, -itum*, "to stir up; to excite."

29.1. sero ... serio: Note the word play (paronomasia); *serio* means "seriously" (adverb).

subvenit: *subveniō* usually means "come to help," but here it means "come to mind, occur (to someone)" (OLD 3).

auxilium civile: *civilis* refers here to Lucius' status as a *civis Romanus*.

interposito venerabili principis nomine: Roman citizens were traditionally able to appeal to the emperor when their rights were violated, particularly their right not to be subjected to physical abuse.

29.2. vicum < *vīcus, -ī*, m., "village."

quempiam < *quispiam, quaepiam, quodpiam*, "a certain."

nundinis celebrem: "thronged with market-day crowds." *nundinae, -ārum*, f. pl.: "market day"; for *celeber, celebris, celebre* used to describe holiday crowds, cf. OLD 2.

turbelas Graecorum < *turbella (turbēla)*, -ae, f., "a little crowd." The nationality of the crowds is mentioned as a contrast to the very Roman appeal that Lucius is about to make.

genuino sermone: "in my native language"; < *genuīnus, -a, -um*, "inborn, native." Lucius means that, though a donkey, he wants to speak the language of humans, his native language. (For interpretations that see this as distinguishing speech in Latin from speech in Greek see van der Paardt.)

29.3. **tantum:** "only, just"; the adverbial use of the accusative of the pronoun *tantum, -tantī*, cf. OLD 8a.

disertum < *disertus, -a, -um*, here "articulate, distinct"; presumably neuter accusative, modifying O.

reliquum ... non potui: The point is that a donkey can say O, but not O Caesar.

29.4. **aspernati** < *aspernor, -ārī, -ātus*, "to repel; to scorn."

absonum < *absonus, -a, -um*, "discordant."

hinc inde: "on one side, on the other" (cf. OLD *inde* 7a).

cribris < *crībrum, -ī*, n., "sieve"; dative with *idoneus*; the sieve was proverbial for its uselessness, due to the legend that the Danaids in Hades were condemned to carrying water in sieves.

Iuppiter ille: "Great Jupiter"; for this use of *ille* to modify Jupiter in particular, cf. OLD 4b.

29.5. **rosae virgines:** *virgō, virginis*, f., can be used as an adjective, in a figurative sense: e.g. *terra virgo* = "virgin territory" (cf. OLD 2c).

29.6. **inhians** < *inhiō, -āre, -āvī, -ātum*, here "to long for, covet" (+ dative).

undantibus < *undō, -āre, -āvī, -ātum*, here "to run with moisture" (OLD 3).

adfecto < *affectō (adfectō), -āre, -āvī, -ātum*, "to attempt."

29.7. **prodirem** < *prōdeō, -īre, -iī, -itum*, "to come forward."

inter manus latronum: translators offer "at the hands of the brigands," but the attested uses of *manus* in this sense are *manu, manibus*, or *per manum* (cf. OLD 8b; cf. also 21); perhaps *manus* is better taken in the sense of "gang" (cf. OLD 22), i.e. "among the bands (generalizing plural) of brigands."

offenderem < *offendō, offendere, offendī, offensum*, here "to encounter, be faced with" (OLD 3c).

indicii < *indicium, -(i)ī*, n., "disclosure, information, evidence (against someone)."

29.8. **et quidem**: *quidem* can be used, especially when preceded by *et*, to introduce a reinforcement or an afterthought: "and what is more" (cf. OLD 5a); such a meaning is not easy here (and the emendation *equidem* has been proposed), but the contrast appears to be between *tunc* (a momentary check on his impulse) and *necessario* (a required one).

necessario: "of necessity, without option"; adverb.

in asini faciem: *in faciem* + genitive means "so as to present the outward appearance" (of a thing); cf. OLD 2a.

frena rodebam: "I was gnawing at the reins," i.e. "I was champing at the bit"; the use of this equestrian idiom, by a human transformed into a donkey, provides a punchline for the whole book.